kids' Ultimate Craft Book

Bead · Crochet · Knot
Braid · Knit · Sew!

Editors of Quarry Books

QUARRY

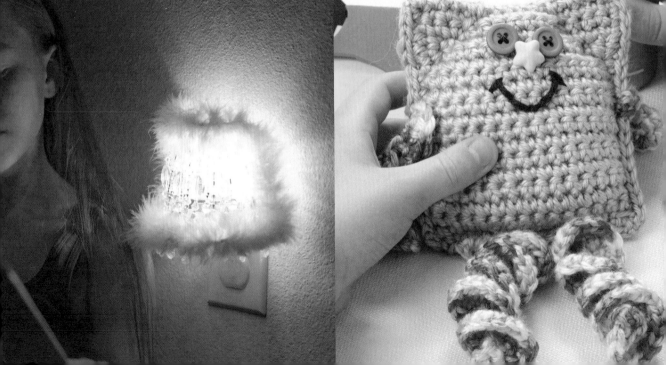

Introduction

Making crafts is a great way to foster creativity, learn new skills, and build confidence. This book does all that and more, with specially selected techniques and projects from five books in the Creative Kids Complete Photo Guide series: *Bead Crafts*, *Braiding & Knotting*, *Crochet*, *Knitting*, and *Sewing*.

Kids will love creating fun jewelry and accessories, eye-catching room décor items, unique stationery, and toys. Among the projects featured from *Bead Crafts* is a chic nightlight shade; from *Braiding & Knotting*, a striking paracord bracelet; from *Crochet*, a colorful granny square scarf; from *Knitting*, an attractive and useful pencil roll; and from *Sewing*, a customizable pillow with a secret pocket. Projects are designed for a range of ages and skill levels, including beginners, and each section includes information on basic techniques, tools, and materials.

Step-by-step instruction and lots of photos help to ensure satisfying results. Besides building creative skills, children will also learn how to read and understand patterns, measure accurately, develop hand-eye coordination, and focus on patience and mindfulness.

Crafting is always more fun with family and friends, and parents can guide and encourage their kids as they discover how far their imaginations can take them. Using materials found around the house can spark ideas and add individuality to finished pieces. Projects make great craft sale items and gifts, and can be personalized with select colors, favorite styles, and handpicked embellishments.

The authors of these books put an enormous amount of expertise and passion into their work, and we'd like to acknowledge their efforts: *Bead Crafts*, Amy Kopperude; *Braiding & Knotting*, Sherri Haab (with Michelle Barnes); *Crochet*, Deborah Burger; *Knitting*, Mary Scott Huff; and *Sewing*, Janith Bergeron and Christine Ecker.

Ready to dive in? Hours of crafty fun start right now!

Bead Crafts

When I first began playing with beads as a child, I had a cardboard box filled with pipe cleaners, yarn, plastic pony beads, buttons, and more. I liked to experiment, but I didn't have anything near the range of supplies that are available today for kids' bead crafts. Walk into any craft store, and the aisles are not only packed with beading and stringing materials, but also cover an experience level ranging from novice to artist. You can be any age, any experience level, with any range of ideas for projects and be absolutely stellar at beading, if only you have an imagination (and sometimes, patience). That's all it takes!

If you can dream, then the gamut of bead crafting is endless. You can start out with large-hole beads like pony beads and work your way toward more intricate glass beads. Some beads, like fusible beads, are rarely strung, but instead melted together to make works of art like drink coasters or window decorations. You can even make your own beads, and *Creative Kids Complete Photo Guide to Bead Crafts* will show you how to do that, too!

If you're just starting out with bead crafts, then stringing beads onto pipe cleaners or jelly cord—and using your fingers to bend, loop, and tie—will be much easier than learning to manipulate various wire gauges with round- and flat-nose pliers. But the more you experiment with new techniques and the more you practice, the better you will get—and the better your final work will be.

Don't let fancy tools and supplies scare you. Many times, you can substitute one tool or supply for another with a little ingenuity. This book will also show you how to use tools ranging from simple household items like scissors and cylinder-shape dowels and bottles to more complex bead craft–specific pliers and snips. In addition, these pages will teach you how to tie parachute cord and jute twine using macramé techniques, how to weave beads onto string by following a pattern, how to make projects ranging from jewelry and accessories to sculptural pieces and decorations, and much more.

The projects in this chapter are designed for both boys and girls at a variety of skill levels, so there's something for everyone. Parents and kids can create together, or parents can be on standby to help with safety steps like ironing or intricate steps like finishing touches. So prepare yourself for hours of creative fun, and let's get started!

—Amy Kopperude

Materials and Tools

You will be amazed by what you can create with so many different kinds of beads which are easily found online and in craft stores. Most craft stores sell variety packs of colorful plastic shape (A) and pony (B) beads. These are excellent for starting out. In addition to being colorful, some of the beads for children are metallic (C), or they can be linked together, as is the case with tri-shape and sunburst beads (D). Fusible beads (E) are placed on a peg board in a pattern and then heated with an iron until they melt together, but they can also be used for bead ing. If you want to work with more natural beads, craft stores also sell wooden and nature-tone beads (F). Glass beads (G) because of their detail and sophistication. Seed beads (H) can be used by experienced and patient crafters for embroidery work. This is only the beginning of what you'll find when you start looking for beads. Specialty shops carry beads made from recycled materials and even mood beads! You might not use all the materials and tools pictured here in the projects that follow, but they are handy to know about for future projects.

C

D

E

F

G

H

The materials and tools on these pages will guide you in understanding what various beadwork items look like and how they are used. The "You Will Need" list of each project includes some of the materials and tools that are described in more detail here. Refer to this section to answer any questions about beading materials. You might not use all the tools and materials listed here, but they are good to know about for future projects.

Wire

Wire comes in various gauges and colors for a variety of projects including beading and wire wrapping. Heavy gauges are more difficult to manipulate and better for wire wrapping than beading because many beads won't fit over the thicker wire. Soft gauge wire is better for more intricate work and for threading beads, but will break if it is manipulated too much.

Coated Wire

Coated wire (e.g., telephone wire) is used to make the Button Ring on page 30, and it can be purchased new from a hardware store or as recycled material online. The striped and colorful wire is very easy for small hands to manipulate without tools and is great for simple projects that require large-hole beads.

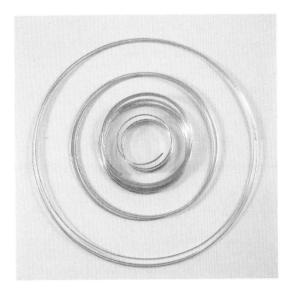

Colored Copper Wire

Copper wire is sold in a variety of colors and gauges. The gauge is important depending on the size of the holes in the beads that are being used for a project. The hard gauges (e.g., typically lower than 22 gauge) require beads with bigger holes and are often more difficult to bend. The soft gauges (e.g., 24, 26, 28) are very easy to bend and often more fragile. Colored copper wire is used to make the Button Ring on page 30, and the Crystal Night-Light Shade on page 34.

Memory Wire

Memory wire is sold in coiled sizes and is used to make preformed necklaces, bracelets, and rings. The circular shape of the wire is resistant to bending, so memory wire is preferred for wrapped jewelry such as the Twirly Whirly Watch Bracelet on page 26.

Strings 'n Things

Beads can be threaded onto many different types of string and cord. Choosing the right fiber for bead threading is essential for the final outcome of a project. Whereas some fibers like jute and nylon are durable; other "fibers"—like jelly cord and pipe cleaners—have elasticity for making bracelets or will bend and conform nicely for shaped projects. Each project identifies exactly what you will need.

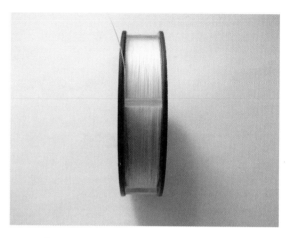

Beading Thread

Nylon beading thread and other fiber threads are best for projects with closely woven beaded rows because the thread responds well to any curves in the beaded strand and produces a nice drape.

Parachute Cord

Parachute cord is a woven nylon cord with some elasticity that comes in sizes that refer to the cord's breaking strength (such as "550 pounds"). The core of the cord is typically made up of several triple-woven strands of yarn surrounded by the nylon sheath. Parachute cord is popular for bulky macramé projects with strong plastic clasps.

Bits 'n Pieces

The bits and pieces you will need for the projects in this book are what many beadwork enthusiasts refer to as "findings." These are the small objects used for linking and attaching beads, thread, and wire.

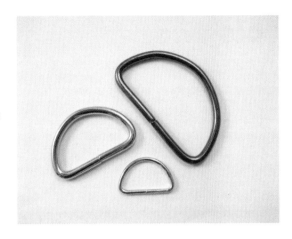

D-Ring

A D-ring is a D-shaped metal ring that comes in a variety of sizes. The straight side of the D-ring is usually attached to a fabric strip, such as at the end of a belt or dog leash.

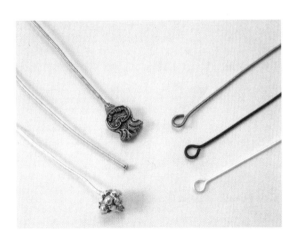

Head Pin or Eye Pin

A head pin is a straight piece of wire with a flat, round, or ornamental end to keep beads from sliding off. An eye pin has one looped end instead of a flat end.

Jump/Split Ring

A jump ring is a looped piece of wire used to connect beaded strands. Split rings are similar to jump rings but the wires overlap.

Tools

You can't make projects with beads without some basic tools for cutting and shaping string and wire. In addition, you'll need tools from around the house like glue or even an iron and an oven to adhere pieces together.

Bead Reamer

A bead reamer is a hand-held tool used to remove obstructions from a bead hole. The reamer is placed inside the hole and twisted back and forth.

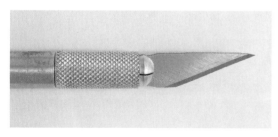

Craft Knife

A craft knife is a small utility knife used for precision cutting. The angled razor blade can be exchanged for a new blade when it becomes dull. A craft knife should be used only by an adult or a young adult under careful supervision.

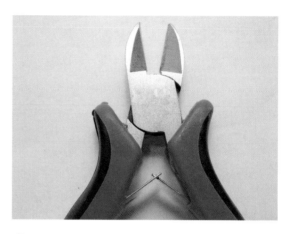

Cutters

Jewelry wire cutters have blades with different angles for different purposes. In general, however, any wire cutters can be used for the projects in this section.

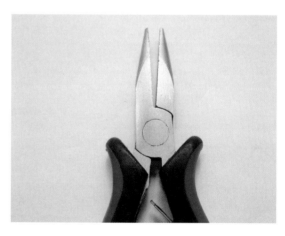

Flat-Nose Pliers

Flat-nose pliers are useful for bending wire at right angles and tightening/flattening coiled wire.

Glue

The projects in this section use a strong craft glue such as Aleene's Tacky Glue. Jewelry glues that require room ventilation or that cannot come into contact with skin are neither necessary nor recommended for these projects.

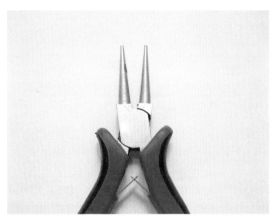

Round-Nose Pliers

Round-nose pliers are used to bend wire into loops and spirals. Refer to the instructions on pages 23 to 24 to learn how to use round-nose pliers. A pencil or dowel can also be used for more pliable wire, like telephone wire, especially for younger children who may have difficulty holding and using the round-nose pliers.

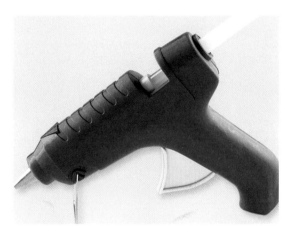

Glue Gun

A crafter's hot glue gun is an electrical tool used to fuse materials together. A cylindrical glue stick (which can be purchased in a package of multiples) is pushed through a chamber at the back of the tool, and hot, melted glue comes out of the nozzle when the trigger is squeezed. A glue gun typically has a metal easel for setting up the tool while it's heating or not in use, and care should be taken not to touch the nozzle or the melted glue while the tool is plugged in. A hot glue gun is used to fuse the white feather boa trim to the night light in the project on page 34.

Scissors

Scissors can be used to cut a multitude of materials: paper, fiber, plastic, even soft-gauge wire. In lieu of wire cutters, scissors can be used for some of the projects in this section. Scissors are an easy cutting instrument for young children and often are the preferred method of cutting.

Techniques

Once you understand the materials and tools necessary for the projects in this chapter, you can learn exactly how to use some of them by applying techniques such as threading beads, macramé tying, and manipulating wire into loops and spirals with different pliers. You may not use all the techniques listed here for the projects in this section, but they're good to know about for future beading projects.

Threading Beads

There are many different gauges of wire, as well as various widths and types of stringing material, so the most important guideline to keep in mind when threading beads is whether the diameter of the bead's hole is big enough for the type of wire, thread, or other material you are using.

Once the correct beads and stringing material have been determined, simply thread the beads onto the stringing material. There may be times when a needle is necessary—for instance, if a bead's hole is rough or slightly obstructed, as may be the case with handmade glass beads.

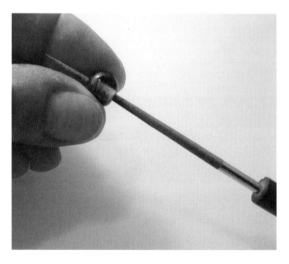

If a bead's hole has an obstruction, use a bead reamer to smooth it away.

Working with Wire

So many jewelry findings are made with wire: head and eye pins, jump rings, ear wires, chain, and more. Some findings can be made with jewelry tools and a handful of techniques. A few of those techniques are described here.

Making Loops and Spirals

Use a pair of round-nose pliers to grip the end of a piece of wire (A), preferably a medium gauge that won't bend too easily but also won't be so thick as to be difficult to work with (22- to 24-gauge should work best). Rotate the pliers, wrapping the wire one full turn around one jaw of the pliers (B). When you have reached one rotation, you have a **loop** for one jump ring. Remove the loop and snip off the excess wire using wire cutters. To make several jump rings, wrap the wire around the jaw of the pliers several times in a tight **spiral** (C). Then remove the spiral and cut through one side (all rows of spiraled wire) to make several jump rings (D). The round-nose pliers are cone shaped, so you can make many different sizes of loops and spirals.

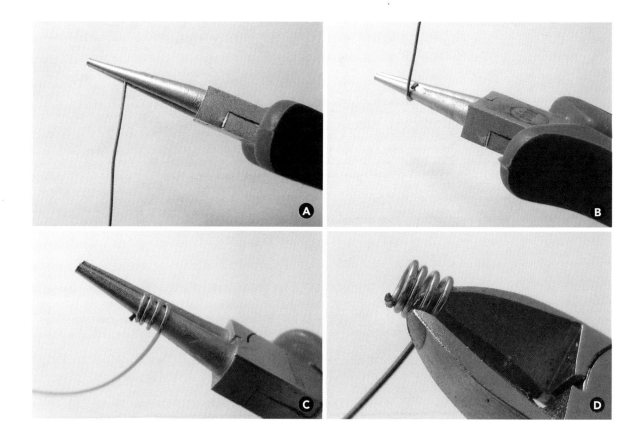

Making Coils

To make a **coil**, grip the wire just as you did for creating a loop and wrap the wire around the very tip of the round-nose pliers so that you have the smallest curve possible (A, B). Once you have a sharp curve in the wire, use a pair of flat-nose pliers to continue to curve your long piece of wire around the sharp curve that you started with. You will need to use your free hand to help bend the wire into a coil (C). The flat-nose pliers will keep the coil flat and together for a uniform look.

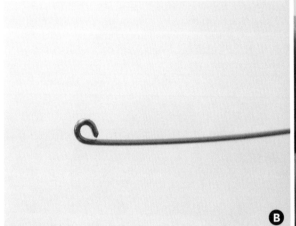

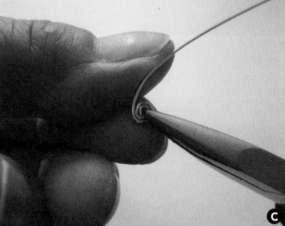

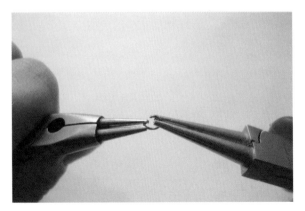

Opening and Closing a Jump Ring

Use two pairs of flat-nose (or other) pliers to grip each side of a jump ring near the opening. Then, bring one hand toward you and the other hand away from you at the same time. Never pull the ring out to the sides because it weakens the wire and distorts the ring. Close the jump ring the same way it was opened.

Twisting Wire Together

Holding two high-gauge (soft) wires together at the ends, use both hands to twist the wires together in the same manner that you would use to close a twist tie on a loaf of bread. Twist to the preferred length.

If you want to add beads to the twisted strand, separate the wires when you have reached a preferred length (A), thread a bead onto just one wire (B), then continue twisting the strands together until you reach the next preferred length (C). Continue threading beads and twisting the wires until the strand is the length you need for your project.

A more challenging way to thread beads onto twisted wire is to start at the stage where you separate your wires, then make a fold in one of the wires (D), slide a bead or beads onto the folded wire (E), twist the folded wire until the twist in the folded strand meets up with the original twisted and beaded strand, and finally, twist the two original wires together (F). Add beads and twist wire until you reach your next preferred length.

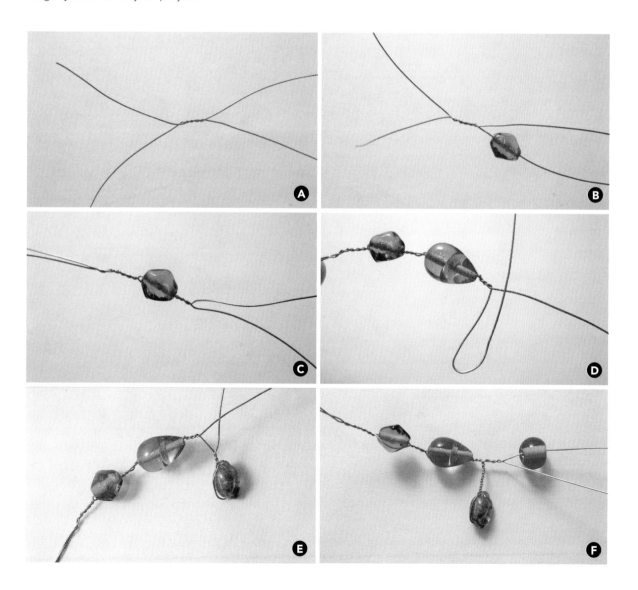

Friendship Charm Pin

Look for charms and colored beads that match your friends' personalities—initials, hobbies, birthstones, favorite colors, school activities—and make detachable charms that can be given away or traded for a collection that can be worn proudly on a jacket, a bag, or shoelaces.

You Will Need

- 1 charm pin or large safety pin
- small decorative beads
- metal charms
- eye pins (one for each hanging charm)
- lobster clasps (one for each hanging charm)
- head pins (one for each beaded strand charm)
- hollow spacer (for holding extra hanging charms)
- wire cutters
- flat-nose pliers
- round-nose pliers

Directions

The following directions are for three different types of hanging charms for a friendship pin, but use your imagination to come up with still dozens more ideas for accessorizing a friendship pin with detachable charms.

1 Choose a charm and add it to the eye of an eye pin by using flat-nose pliers to open and close the eye with the charm in place (refer to the instructions for a jump ring on page 18).

2 Add beads to the eye pin, but leave approximately ¼" (6 mm) of the wire unbeaded. Use wire cutters to trim any excess wire.

3 Use the round-nose pliers to create a loop with the excess wire of the eye pin. Before closing the loop, thread a lobster clasp onto the wire, making sure the opening of the clasp faces the back of the charm (A). Use the flat-nose pliers to close the loop (B). This completes one charm.

4 To make a beaded strand charm, start with step 2 but add the beads to a head pin, not an eye pin (A). Then, leave ¼" (6 mm) of the pin unbeaded to make the loop (B) and attach the lobster clasp.

(continued)

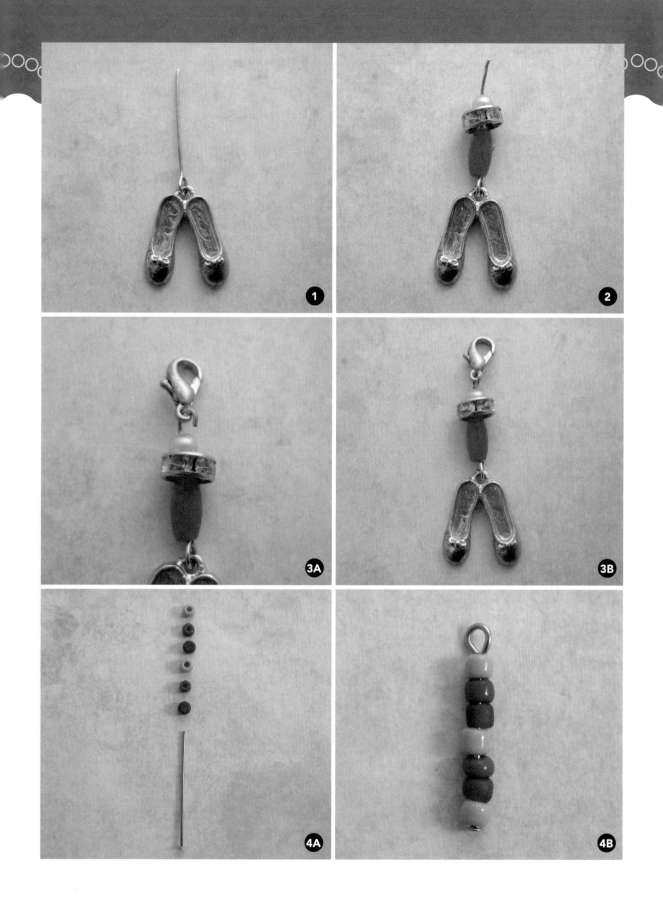

1

2

3A

3B

4A

4B

5 To make a charm using a hollow spacer for hanging extra charms, use two head pins. Thread the head pins through each end of the spacer from the inside out. The head pin designated for the top of the charm will get trimmed to ¼" (6 mm) and then looped to attach the lobster clasp. The head pin designated for the bottom of the charm will get trimmed to ¼" (6 mm) and then looped to attach a charm (A). If the head pins are too small for the spacer holes and pull through the holes, thread a seed bead onto each head pin before threading it through the spacer holes, and that will keep the head pins in place (B).

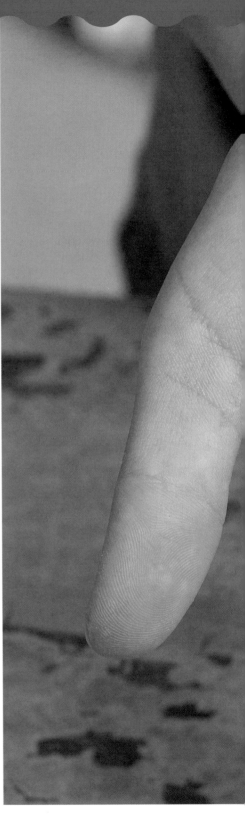

You Will Need

- 4 to 5 coils of bracelet memory wire

- assorted beads and spacers

- 2 medium jump rings

- 1 small jump ring

- 1 watch face with top and bottom loops (pendant holes) (found in craft stores)

- 1 hook clasp

- round-nose pliers

- wire cutters

- *Optional:* one or two 6" (15 cm) pieces of thin organza ribbon

Twirly Whirly Watch Bracelet

The Twirly Whirly Watch Bracelet can be created in styles ranging from fun to sophisticated. Use colorful acrylic beads for a youthful look and glass or metal beads for a fashionable flair.

Directions

1 Attach the medium jump rings to the top and bottom loops of the watch face, following instructions for opening and closing jump rings on page 18.

2 Attach the small jump ring to the medium jump ring through the top loop of the watch face. Attach the hook clasp to the small jump ring.

(continued)

3 Use the round-nose pliers to create a loop at one end of the memory wire. Attach the looped memory wire to the jump ring that runs through the bottom loop of the watch face so that the outside coil of the wire is facing out along with the watch face.

4 Begin beading the memory wire. Alternate styles and sizes of beads until the bracelet coils twice around the wrist. Keep in mind that the hook at the top of the watch face is the closure that attaches to the opposite end of the memory wire once it has been beaded and coiled around the wrist, so stop beading the memory wire when the top of the watch meets up with the end of the beaded memory wire. *Note:* Wrap the wire around your wrist to judge how long to bead the memory wire.)

5 When the coils are the preferred length, use the wire cutters to cut the excess memory wire so that ½" (13 mm) remains.

6 Use the round-nose pliers to create a sideways loop. To put on the bracelet, attach the hook clasp in the top of the watch to the sideways loop of the memory wire. The bracelet should be slightly loose like a bangle.

7 *Optional:* Tie one or two pieces of 6" (15 cm) organza ribbon through the jump rings above and below the watch face to fill in the gaps where there are no beads.

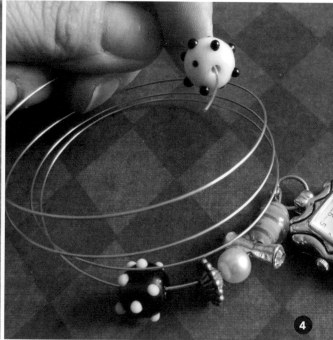

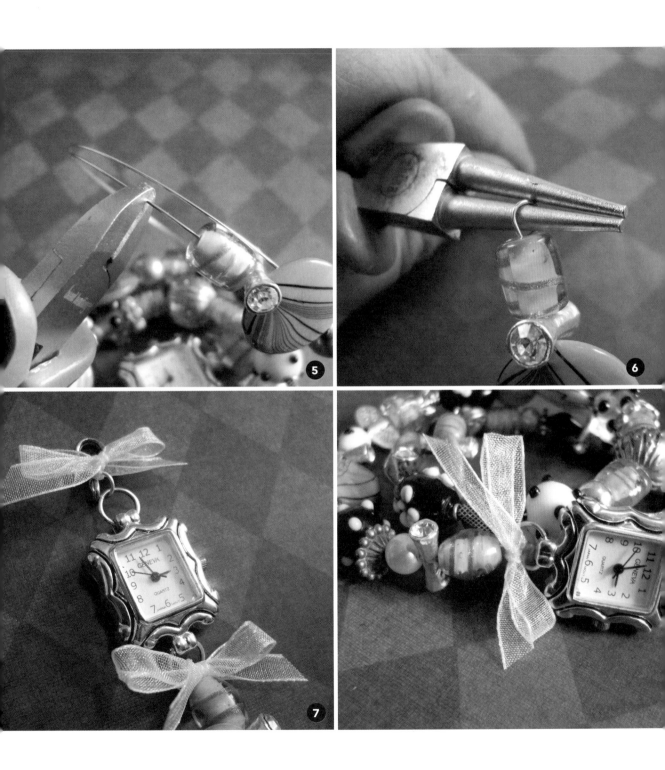

Button Ring

Make this quick piece of finger bling with colorful coated wire and assorted multicolored buttons stacked like a flower and accented with tiny bead baubles.

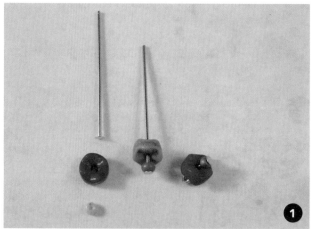

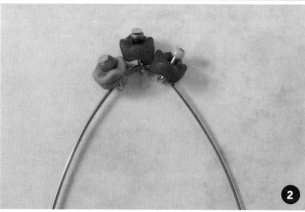

Directions

1 Make three tiny bead charms for the top of the button ring by threading one seed bead and one flower bead onto a head pin, using wire cutters to trim the excess wire back to ¼" (6 mm) and using round-nose pliers to create a small closed loop at the end of the head pin. (See page 17 for creating a loop with round-nose pliers.)

2 Find the halfway point of the 6" (15 cm) piece of wire and thread the beaded head pins to the halfway point.

(continued)

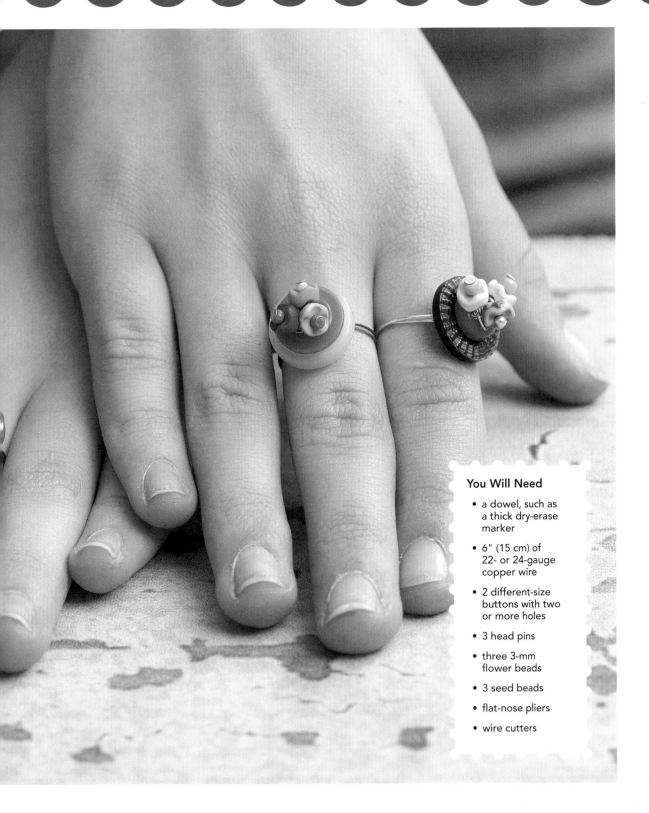

You Will Need

- a dowel, such as a thick dry-erase marker

- 6" (15 cm) of 22- or 24-gauge copper wire

- 2 different-size buttons with two or more holes

- 3 head pins

- three 3-mm flower beads

- 3 seed beads

- flat-nose pliers

- wire cutters

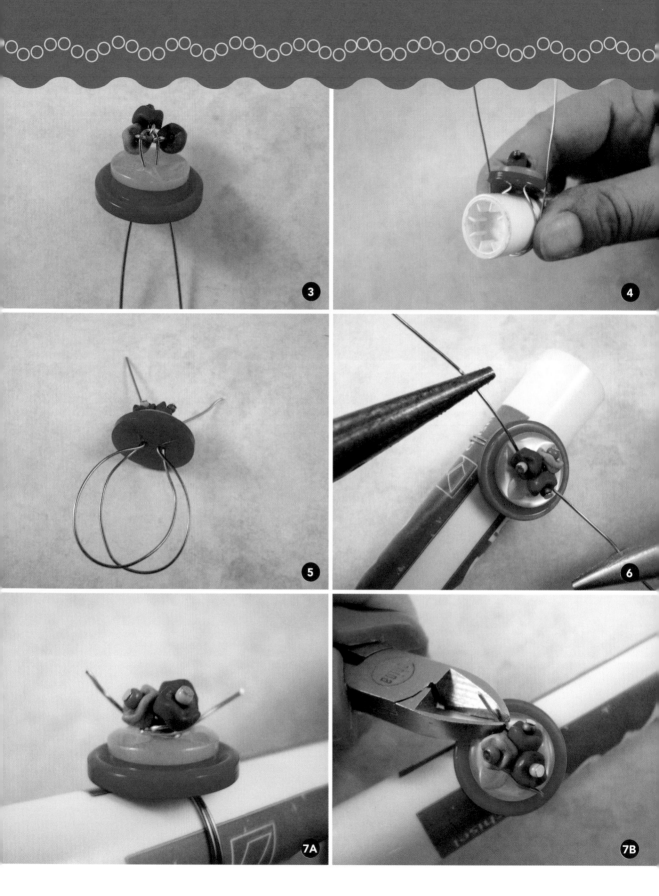

3 Stack two different-color, different-size buttons together. Then, run each end of wire down through each of the two holes in the buttons, keeping the beaded head pins on the central part of the wire.

4 Use a thick marker or a dowel that is about the thickness of a finger for wrapping the wire. Hold the buttons against the marker and bring each wire from one side around to the other side, then straight up.

5 Remove the ring from the marker to insert the two wire ends up through the button holes they are facing.

6 Return the ring to the marker. Then, use two pairs of flat-nose pliers (even round-nose pliers will work) to pull the two wires tightly up through the buttonholes and out to the sides. This will tighten the wires and make them more uniformly round.

7 Wrap each wire end tightly around the base of the cluster of beaded head pins (A), and use wire cutters to trim off the excess wire (B).

Crystal Night-Light Shade

This sophisticated night-light shade is a simple way to dress up a girl's bedroom. Crystal beads will cast soothing rainbows on the wall and drive away nighttime fears.

You Will Need

- 1 round night-light shade kit (lampshop.com)
- approximately twenty 6" (15 cm) pieces of 24-gauge silver-colored wire
- approximately twenty 4" (10 cm) strands of clear and crystal beads in varying widths and styles
- 9 crystal drop beads
- 21" (53 cm) of white feather trim
- wire cutters
- hot-glue gun

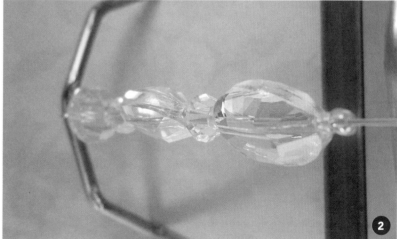

Directions

1 Work from the center of the night-light shade. Use your fingers to wrap one piece of 6" wire around the top metal rod of the shade and twist into place.

2 Thread a variety of beads onto the wire until they reach the bottom metal rod of the shade. Wrap and twist the remaining wire into place the same way as before. Use wire cutters to remove any excess wire.

(continued)

3 Follow steps 1 and 2 to bead more wires on either side of the center wire. Work from the center to the outside edge to be sure you balance the beads. When you are finished, look for spaces between strands of beads that are wide enough for another strand, and add strands as necessary. Use smaller beads to fill in open spaces so that the strands don't crowd each other.

4 When the shade is filled in with strands of beads, secure the crystal drop beads, evenly spaced, to the bottom rod of the shade with jump rings (A, B). See page 18 if you need to review how to open and close jump rings.

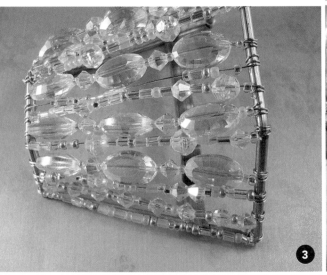

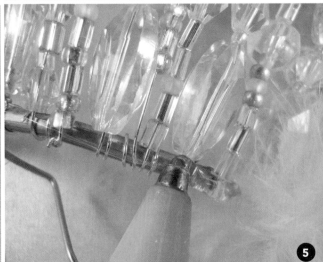

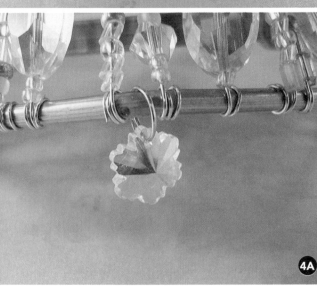

5 Have an adult hot glue the white feather trim to the shade, working across the top rod of the shade, down the side, across the bottom rod of the shade, and up the opposite side. This will hide all of the twisted wire ends and keep the crystal drop beads from sliding back and forth.

6 Use scissors along the bottom inside edge of the night-light shade to trim back the feathers so that the crystal drop beads are visible when hanging.

Braiding and Knotting

The art of knotting and braiding has ancient roots. Knots were used for many utilitarian purposes, such as the most basic skill needed to tie a fish net or construct a trap to gather food. Knots are a big part of maritime history, as they were used for so many practical purposes for life on the sea. Sailors learned how to tie knots out of necessity but would also tie decorative knot patterns with the same basic knots that evolved for macramé. Even the term *knots*, which is still used to describe the speed of a boat, originated from the practice of sailors tying knots at regular intervals to measure distances traveled by sea. You will find knotting and braiding part of every culture and throughout history. A trip to a museum will most likely yield samples of knotting or braiding in some form or another.

The fun thing about knotting and braiding is that the same knots that were tied in ancient times are still used today. There are a few basic knots that are universally known and will allow you to make a number of combinations to complete all kinds of projects. This section contains the basic instructions to tie fundamental knots and braids along with fun projects to make using them.

I remember the first macramé projects I made in the 1970s. Our community offered craft classes in the neighborhood and I signed up to make a macramé plant hanger. I still remember going to the hardware store with my mother to buy the required "ceiling tile" on the supply list. I didn't know what a ceiling tile was, but it turned out to be a dense foam square. This was the preferred work surface for tying macramé knots because you could push pins into it. You would line up all the cords on the board and then proceed to tie elaborate knot patterns, pinning knots to the board along the way with heavy T-pins. This kept the knots neat and organized. The plant hanger took me a long time to complete, but I was pretty proud of my creation. It was made using hot pink jute with white beads. I hung it in my room and filled it with a spider plant, a hugely popular houseplant back in the day. I went on to make a few more plant hangers and a few pieces of jewelry. I was probably about ten years old when I went through my macramé phase and didn't tie knots for years afterward, but the skill of tying knots stuck with me. It's like riding a bike; once you begin knotting again, it all comes back.

When I started making jewelry as an adult, I gravitated toward designs incorporating fiber and knots. Visually, I found mixed media exciting; I enjoyed knotting fibers with metal, clay, or beads. With the popularity of beading and jewelry making in recent years, stringing materials emerged that hadn't been available in the past. This added to my desire to incorporate fiber and to bring those former macramé skills back to good use.

There are many options for stringing materials available on the market today. This variety allows for a wide range of possibilities for projects. You can find everything from jewelry-making string to heavier materials such as nylon cord. It's easy to find the supplies to make a wearable, such as a necklace or bracelet. With heavy nylon cord, you can make a survival bracelet, pet leash, or a household item. Knotted items such as key chains or covered earbuds make great gifts. Once you learn the basic knots, you can create your own original designs. Knotting and braiding are fun for all ages and make great family activities.

—*Sherri Haab*

Materials and Tools

Almost any type of thread, string, or cord may be used for knotting and braiding. It all depends on the project you are making. Embroidery floss (**1**), nylon bead cord (**2**), heavy nylon parachute cord (paracord) (**3**), hemp (**4**), cotton (**5**), and leather (**6**) are just a few examples of knotting materials.

Embroidery floss and nylon bead cord work very well for delicate jewelry pieces and other projects where you need fine cord to fit through small beads. Embroidery floss is available in every color imaginable and, best of all, it is inexpensive! Embroidery floss is a longtime favorite for friendship bracelets. Look for floss in craft and fabric stores. Nylon bead cord comes in a variety of colors and is available in different thicknesses. This cord is commonly used for beading and macramé and is sold in bead shops. This cord doesn't stretch or fray easily. The ends can be finished with heat to melt the nylon, which will prevent fraying. Fine nylon bead cord will fit through small beads, making it a good choice for projects where bead hole size is an issue.

All-purpose nylon cord is manufactured in several weights and weaves. One type is commonly known as paracord and was originally used to suspend parachutes. Paracord is the popular material used to make survival bracelets, which are both utilitarian and fashionable. The cord is thick and makes a nice heavy bracelet. It is available in several weights or thicknesses and in a variety of colors and patterns. Paracord was used to make the bracelet on page 60 and the Dog Leash project on page 70. Other types of heavy nylon cord are good to use for larger projects. Nylon is easy to melt with a thread melting tool, which helps when joining colors or finishing cord ends. Look in the general supply department at craft stores for heavy nylon cord.

Other knotting materials, such as cotton, leather, jute, and hemp, will give you creative design options. One of these materials might offer the particular color, thickness, or texture that is just right for the project you are working on. Use jewelry cement or white glue to seal the ends of cords that are not made from nylon and cannot be melted. Craft and fabric stores carry all kinds of cords that might inspire you with a new idea. You might not use all the materials and tools pictured here in the projects that follow, but they are handy to know about for future projects.

Beads and Findings

Findings are the necessary hardware parts you will need for certain projects. Key rings, buckles, and other fasteners are examples of findings that are not only necessary for the function of the overall design, but are also there to serve as an anchor to which cords are tied. Hardware or general variety stores are good places to look for the larger items, such as key rings and spring hooks. For jewelry projects, clasps, jump rings, beads, and charms are available from beading supply and craft stores. Hardware and beads really add to knotted patterns to make them extraordinary. They add texture and color to complement the knots and provide neat finishes for cord ends. Here are a sampling that are used in these projects:

Key rings: Split rings (**1**) and swivel-eye snap hooks (**2**) are great for making key rings or providing attachment points. A swivel-type hook was used in the Dog Leash project, to name one example. Rings and hooks can be used to make detachable cord designs for many applications.

Chain: Weave a chain (**3**) or strand of rhinestones into the knot work of a bracelet to add extra sparkle and structure.

Jump rings and clasps: Jump rings (**4**) and clasps (**5**) are jewelry findings that are usually carried in craft and bead shops. Jump rings provide a way to attach charms to braided designs. Lobster-claw clasps are particularly good to use in conjunction with cord designs where a strong clasp is needed.

Beads: Seed beads with large holes (**6**) will pass through nylon bead cord. "E" beads (**7**) are extra-large seed beads (6 mm size). Large wooden and plastic beads (**8**) with large holes are longtime favorites used for macramé. These beads will fit over paracord nylon to decorate a survival bracelet, or they can be used over heavier cord to add interest to a plant hanger or wall hanging.

Natural and found objects: Wooden sticks, seashells (**9**), and even hardware parts can be incorporated into a knotted or braided pattern to add interest and texture.

Tools and Supplies

Most of the tools you will need to get started are common items you might already have. Here is a list of a few basic tools and supplies that you will need:

Scissors: Basic tools needed for working with thread and cord include a pair of sharp scissors for cutting. For heavy nylon cord, wire cutters are a good substitute for scissors.

Clipboard: A clipboard that can be purchased from an office supply store is handy for anchoring or holding threads. This provides an easy work surface that is portable, too.

Corkboard: A small cork bulletin board makes a good surface to pin cords to for complex projects.

Pins: T-pins hold cord in place on the corkboard.

Fine wire: Use a small piece of fine wire bent in half for stringing thread through beads.

Tape: Tape helps hold core threads taut as you tie knots.

Needle tool: A needle tool or an awl is useful for unpicking knots in thread when you make a mistake.

Ruler: Use a ruler or measuring tape to measure your cords and threads for projects.

Melting tool: A thread melting tool is a battery-operated heating tool that will melt nylon cord. Melted nylon pieces will adhere to each other to join cords or to hide stray cords. This tool will also melt and seal the frayed ends of nylon to keep it from raveling. Thread melting tools are available through bead and jewelry-making suppliers.

Glue: Clear jewelry cement and white glue will dry clear over cords and threads. Use glue to seal cord ends or to keep thread from unraveling.

Toothpicks: Use toothpicks to apply glue to cord or to separate strands of thread and cord.

Binder Clips: Use clips from the office supplystore to help hold wound string or thread. This is especially helpful when working on a complicated project with cords that easily tangle.

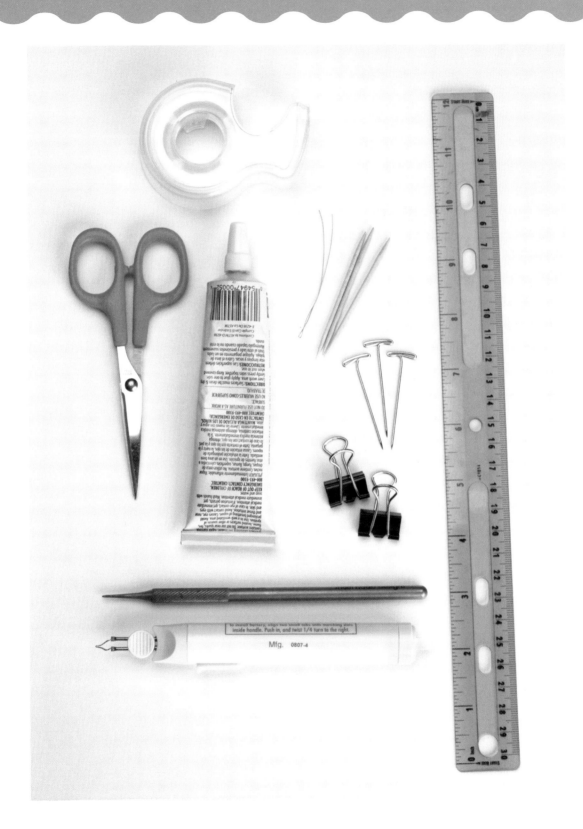

Techniques

Starting

To begin a knotted or braided design you will need to secure your cords in two ways. First, you will need to anchor the cords to something that will hold the cords with tension so you can tie and weave the fibers. Pin or tape cords to a corkboard or table so you can begin knotting. An office clipboard also works very well to hold cords. The clipboard makes it easy to remove the work if you need to make frequent adjustments. Second, you will need to secure your cords by physically binding them together as a means to organize them to begin a pattern. Here are a few knotting ideas for starting and securing cords:

Overhand knots: To secure cords, a simple overhand knot holds everything together. This knot can be used to start and end a knotted pattern for a bracelet, for example. The overhand knot makes a nice, neat finish for cord ends. Overhand knots also keep beads from slipping off the cord. See page 46 for instructions.

Braided loop: Braid three or more threads at the center of your work consisting of long lengths of cut threads. Braid them for a short length and then form a loop with the braided section by bringing the threads together. Tie a knot to secure the base of the loop before proceeding with your knotted pattern.

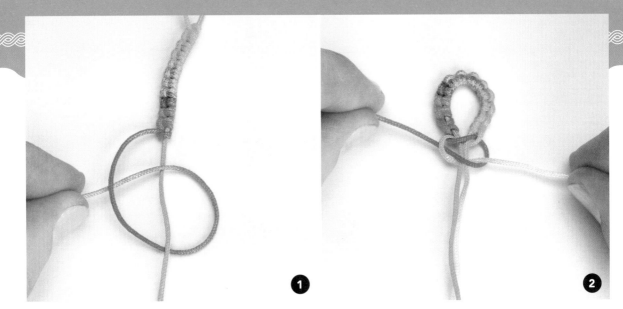

Lark's head loop: This loop has a neat, professional look that works well for starting a pattern in which you will need to hang or fasten something. This is one way to start a bracelet or necklace. After completing a bracelet or necklace design, you can tie loose cord ends through the lark's head loop to fasten.

1   Start at the middle of your work by doubling the cords. Tie a series of lark's head knots (see page 59) using one long cord. Tie it over a core of one or more cords or threads. Tie a series of knots until the section is long enough to form a loop. The thread that is used for tying the knots will become shorter than the core threads, so if needed cut this particular thread longer than the rest so you won't run short later on.

2   Fasten the base of the loop with a square knot (see page 54), which will keep the work nice and flat.

Finishing

There are several options for finishing the ends of a project, depending on the design you are creating. Some finishing techniques are needed to provide an attachment or closure, such as loose ties for a bracelet. Other finishing methods are needed to secure the end of a cord or keep threads from unraveling. Here are a few techniques:

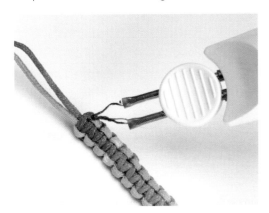

Heat: After you complete a project, you may need to seal the cut ends of cord or thread. If you are using a nylon fiber such as paracord, the nylon will melt with heat, which will keep it from raveling. You can melt loose fibers close to a knot, which will seamlessly hide any frayed ends.

Glue: To finish fibers other than nylon you can use a jewelry cement or white glue to seal the ends of the cord. Dip the cut ends of the cord into the glue and then let the glue dry. This will help keep the fibers sealed so they won't ravel.

Braiding: Instead of simply leaving loose threads to finish the end of a bracelet, you can braid the threads. If you have six or more loose threads, divide them into two groups and braid each group to create two braided strands to be used as ties. Finish the braided ends with overhand knots. Tie the braided strands through a loop at the other end of the bracelet to fasten.

Adjustable square knot slide: This knot is used to secure the end cords of a bracelet or necklace so that it is easy to put on and take off and to make it adjustable so that the piece will fit perfectly. After you finish a piece of jewelry, use the loose tail ends as your base to tie a slide knot over. Bring the loose thread ends toward each other and then overlap them. Use a 12-inch (30.5 cm) scrap of thread to tie the adjustable knot. This will make the bracelet adjustable. To tie the knot, tie a few square knots in a row over the core of threads. Trim off the ends of the square knot threads and the loose core threads. Glue or seal the cut ends with heat, depending on the material used.

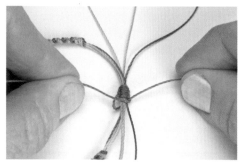

Wrapped finishing knot: A wrapped knot is a coiled knot that is used to bind two or more cords together. For example, it is used for the Plant Hanger project to wrap the cords at the top of the hanger and then used again to bind all of the cords together at the base. To make a wrapped loop:

1 Gather or bundle the cords you wish to wrap. Use a separate cord to do the wrapping with. Fold the wrapping cord to make a loop. Hold this folded cord next to the bundle of cords you wish to wrap.

2 Start wrapping the wrapping cord over itself and around the bundle, wrapping tightly toward the fold or (loop).

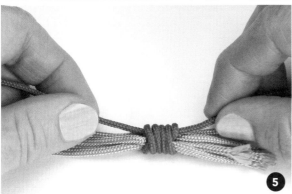

3   Leave a tail of cord showing where you started wrapping, as you will need to pull it later. After wrapping around the bundle several times, pass the wrapping cord through the loop, as shown.

4   Keep tension on both ends as you begin to pull the cord on the right. As you pull, the cord will tighten and bury the loop on the left inside the wrap. Pull the cord on the left to tighten.

5   Pull both ends at the same time. Clip the ends and seal with heat or glue, depending on the fiber.

Knotting Tips

Dampen cords and threads before starting. This helps straighten and soften the fibers, making them easier to knot and braid.

Wind up long cords and hold them with binder clips or rubber bands. Then unwind the cord as you need it.

If cord or thread is hard to pass through a bead or becomes frayed, cut the end at an angle. It also helps to twist the cord in the direction of the twist of the fiber.

If you run out of cord, tie a new piece to your cord and hide the knot under a bead. If you are using nylon, use a thread melting tool to join the cord ends. Loose ends can also be woven into existing knot work to hide them.

To figure out how much cord or thread you need, measure a scrap piece of cord and tie a small section of knots. This will let you determine how much cord was used for that section. Multiply that section by the length of your project to determine how much you will need. Some knots use a lot more cord than others, and it can be tricky to gauge without tying a sample.

Use a needle tool or a toothpick to undo knots. Because nylon is slippery, it is easy to unknot.

Three-Strand Braid

A braid creates a pattern by weaving threads together rather than knotting them. You can use single threads or multiple fibers, dividing them into three sections for a thicker braid.

1 To weave a braid with three threads, tie the threads together and pull them down next to each other. Bring the left thread (blue) over the center thread (green); this thread (blue) now becomes the center.

2 Bring the right thread (yellow) over the center thread (blue); now the yellow thread becomes the center. To proceed, bring the green thread over the yellow. Repeat the pattern by alternating left and right threads, each time crossing over the center thread to form the braid.

Four-Strand Braid

Tie four threads together and number them 1 through 4 from left to right (blue, yellow, green, purple).

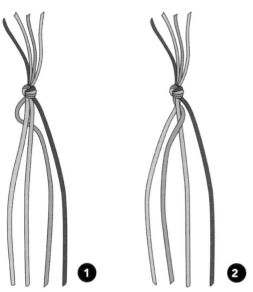

1 Pull the first thread (blue) behind the two threads in the middle (second yellow and third green).

2 Bring the same thread (blue) back over the third thread (green), placing it between the yellow and green threads (yellow on the left and green on the right of the blue thread).

3 Now go to the right side and pull the fourth thread (purple) behind the two center threads.

4 Bring the same (purple) thread back over the blue thread, placing it between the blue and green threads and pulling taut to tighten the threads as you go. Continue the pattern by alternating sides, wrapping behind the center two threads and then around to the center between those threads each time.

Overhand Knot

This is the knot used to secure threads together before beginning a knot pattern or to finish off the ends.

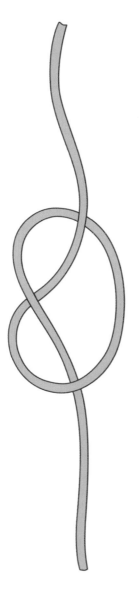

1 Make a loop with one thread (or a group of threads) and bring the end of the thread(s) through the loop, pulling tight.

Half-Knot

This knot is formed with four threads. Tie them together with an overhand knot. The half-knot will form a spiral pattern when tied over and over with a series of knots.

1 Pull two of the threads (blue) straight down to serve as the center core. Place the other two cords out to each side (yellow on the left and green on the right).

2 Bring the thread from the left (yellow) and pull it over the two core threads (blue) to resemble the number 4.

3 Pick up the thread from the right (green) and pass it over the tail of the yellow thread, under the blue core threads, then up through the left yellow loop, as shown. Pull both outside threads taut while keeping the core stationary and tight.

NOTE: If you keep tying the half-knot over and over it forms a twisted pattern around the core. Flip your work over as you progress, as the twist forces you to work around to the back of the core.

Square Knot

The square knot consists of two opposite half-knots. The first half-knot is tied by starting with the thread on the left and then a second half-knot is tied by starting on the right. Tie four threads together using two in the center to serve as the core.

1 Follow the directions for the half-knot to begin the first half of the knot, beginning with the thread on the left, as shown in the illustration (half-knot).

2 Tie another half-knot directly under it, but this time start with the thread on the right. Bring the right (yellow) thread across the two core threads, to look like a backward 4.

3 Now bring the left (green) thread over the tail of the yellow thread you just pulled over from the right. Bring it under the core threads and back up through the loop on the right side. Pull both sides snug around the core.

NOTE: You can tie a square knot without core threads as a finish knot or to secure threads. Tie in the same fashion but without the core threads.

Alternating Square Knot

This knot uses a minimum of six threads, but you can use more to create a wider pattern. Use an even numbers of threads for a neater look. In this example, there are three colors of thread used. The threads were then doubled to give six total to work with. The colors can be arranged in different orders to change the overall appearance of the finished project.

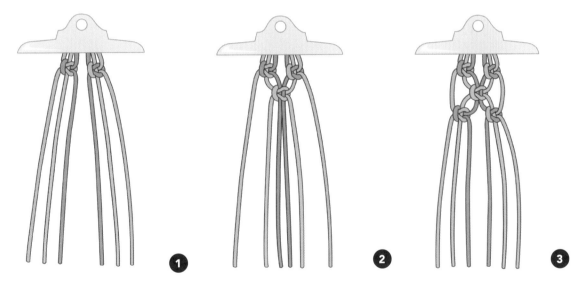

1. Line up six threads across, matching the outside, middle, and inside thread colors as shown. Tie a square knot with three threads on the left and another square knot with the three threads on the right.

2. For the next row, bring the two middle (blue) threads together to serve as the core for the next knot. Tie a square knot with the (yellow) threads over the blue core. Now you will have one square knot in the center.

3. For the third row, tie a square knot with the three threads on the left and then another square knot on the right as you did in step 1. Continue the pattern by alternating steps 1 and 2.

Half-Hitch Knot

The half-hitch knot is a basic fundamental loop knot that is used often. It will form a spiral pattern when tied in a series on its own. It also serves as the foundation for other knots such as the double half-hitch knot, lark's head knot, and the alternating half-hitch knot.

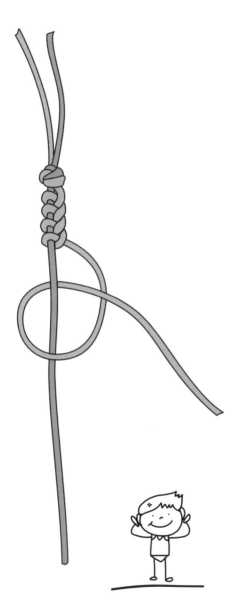

1 Tie the two threads together. One thread will serve as the core while the other ties all of the knots. Bring the (blue) core thread straight down and hold taut. Bring the other thread (green) to the right side; this is the thread that will be doing all of the work and tying the knots. Loop this thread over and around the blue core thread, exiting to the right as shown in the illustration.

2 Pull the green thread tightly around the blue thread. Keep the blue thread taut and straight. This completes the knot.

NOTE: A spiral pattern will appear as you continue tying knots down the core. Flip your work over to follow the knots around as you tie.

The half-hitch knot can also be tied left to right.

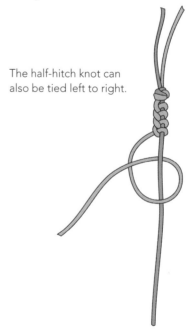

Double Half-Hitch Knot

This knot is commonly referred to as the "friendship bracelet knot." It is simply a half-hitch knot tied twice over a core thread. It can be tied from left to right or from right to left. To make a friendship bracelet, one common thread is tied over single threads. As an alternative, individual threads may be tied over a single common core. The friendship variation forms individual single knots using two threads, whereas the common core variation looks like a wrapped row of knots.

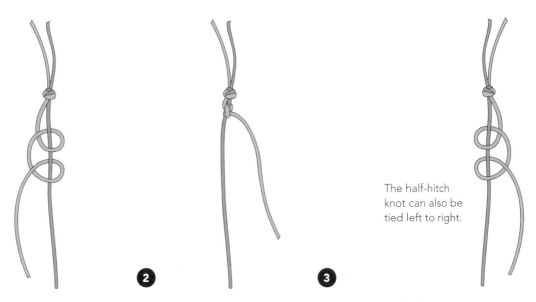

The half-hitch knot can also be tied left to right.

1   Tie the two threads together. One thread will serve as the core while the other ties all of the knots. Bring the (blue) core thread straight down and hold taut. Bring the other thread (green) to the left side; this is the thread that will be doing all of the work and tying the knots. Loop this thread over and around the blue core thread, exiting to the left as shown on the first top loop in the illustration.

2   Pull the first green loop tightly around the blue core thread. Repeat the same loop, wrapping the green thread over the blue core and through to the left as you did in step 1.

3   As you are pulling the thread around to finish the second loop from step 2, pull tight around the core. As you tighten, you will pull the green thread to the right side. The knot will snap into place and the threads will have switched places from where they started. This illustration shows how the finished knot will appear with the blue thread on the left and the green thread on the right. As you practice, the second loop and finished knot will be tied in one continuous motion, making a neatly formed double half-hitch knot.

Alternating Half-Hitch Knot

The secret to this knot is all about keeping tension on the correct thread. It switches back and forth. First, one thread is held tight while the other thread loops around it. Then it switches so that the previously looped thread becomes the new core thread. Pull tight after each loop before beginning the next. The illustration depicts two loose loops to show progression, but in reality the green loop will be tight before tying the last blue loop shown.

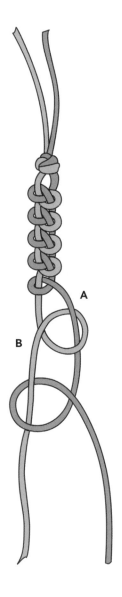

1   Tie the two threads together. Each thread will take turns serving as the core while the other ties the knot. Bring one of the threads down to serve as the core, holding firm (see the blue thread at A). Bring the other thread (green) from the left side and loop this thread over and around the blue core thread, exiting to the left as shown in the illustration.

2   Pull the green thread tightly around the blue thread. Keep the blue thread taut and straight. For the next loop, switch the core to the green thread and hold taut (see B). Wrap the blue thread from the right over and around the green core, exiting to the right as shown at B. Pull tight around the green core.

3   Switch back by pulling the blue thread tight to serve as the core for the next knot. Tie the green thread around it. Keep switching thread tensions and loops back and forth to form the alternating pattern.

Lark's Head Knot

A lark's head knot is a versatile knot, which is used in several ways. It can be used to anchor cords to a foundation to begin a project. For example it is used to attach cords to a key chain loop. It can also be used to tie a pattern. The knot consists of two mirror-image half-hitch knots tied next to each other.

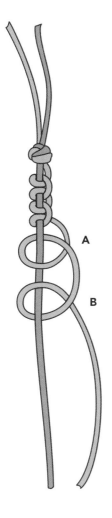

1   Tie the two threads together. One thread will serve as the core while the other ties all of the knots. Bring the (blue) core thread straight down and hold taut. Bring the other thread (green) to the right side; this is the thread that will be doing all of the work and tying the knots. Loop this thread *over* and around the blue core thread, exiting to the right as shown at A.

2   Pull tight around the core. For the next loop, pass the green thread *under* the blue core and then around the core, exiting through to the right as shown at B. Pull tight to complete the knot. Each knot requires two complete loops; the first loop goes over and then the second loop goes under.

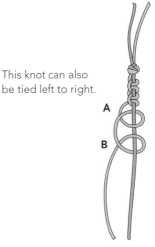

This knot can also be tied left to right.

Survival (Paracord) Bracelet

Paracord gets its name from the cord that was originally used to suspend parachutes. This cord is strong and useful for many purposes. Paracord bracelets are also referred to as "survival bracelets" because the cord has a reputation for survival applications (lashing poles together, water rescue, sewing, or making a fishing line, just to name a few). These bracelets have become popular as a fashion statement. The cord is now available in a variety of colors and patterns. The bracelets are bold and bright. Wear your favorite team or school colors by knotting two bold colors together to make a bracelet!

You will need

- 4 feet (1.2 m) #95 blue nylon paracord
- 3 feet (0.9 m) #95 neon yellow nylon paracord
- paracord clasp or buckle, small size
- thread melting tool

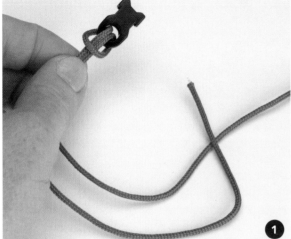

DIRECTIONS

1 Fold the longer (blue) cord 10 inches (25 cm) from the end and form a lark's head knot (see page 59) to attach to one half of the buckle.

2 Slide the cord ends through the other half of the buckle and measure the cords from buckle to buckle to equal the length of your wrist plus about 1 inch (2.5 cm) to determine where to attach the buckle. You will have two cords running down the length of the bracelet that will serve as the core for the knotting.

3 Trim the short tail of the blue cord about 1 inch (2.5 cm) from the base of the buckle. This short cord will be fused to the neon yellow color. Fuse the ends of the blue and neon yellow cords together by rubbing a thread melting tool over the cut ends to meld them.

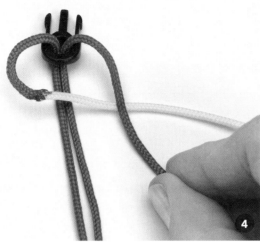

4 Tie a square knot over the center core cords under the buckle with the loose cords. Bring the cord from the left side over to look like the number 4 to begin the knot.

5 Bring the other long cord from the right side over the tail coming from the left cord and pass it up under the core cords and out through the loop on the left to complete a half-knot as shown on page 53.

6 Pull the knot tight under the buckle.

(continued)

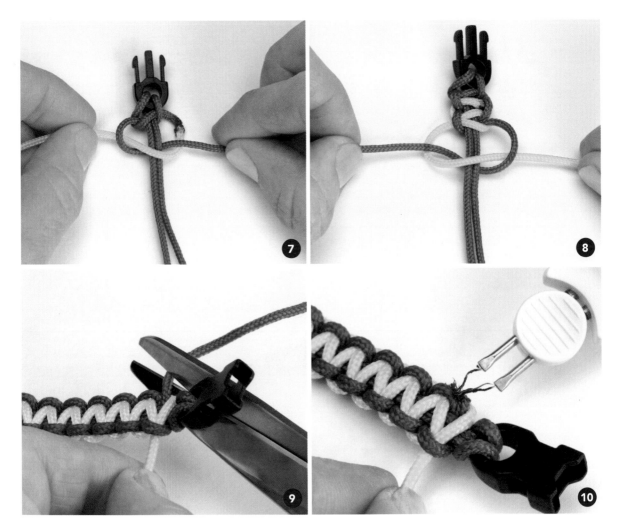

7   Take the cord on the right side and tie the next half-knot to complete a
    full square knot as shown on page 54. This knot is tied using the cord from
    the right side. The knot is a mirror opposite from the first half-knot you
    just tied.

8   Tie a series of square knots over the core cords until you reach
    the end of the bracelet.

9   Cut off the ends of the cords.

10 Seal the cut ends by melting them onto the surrounding knots with a
    thread melting tool.

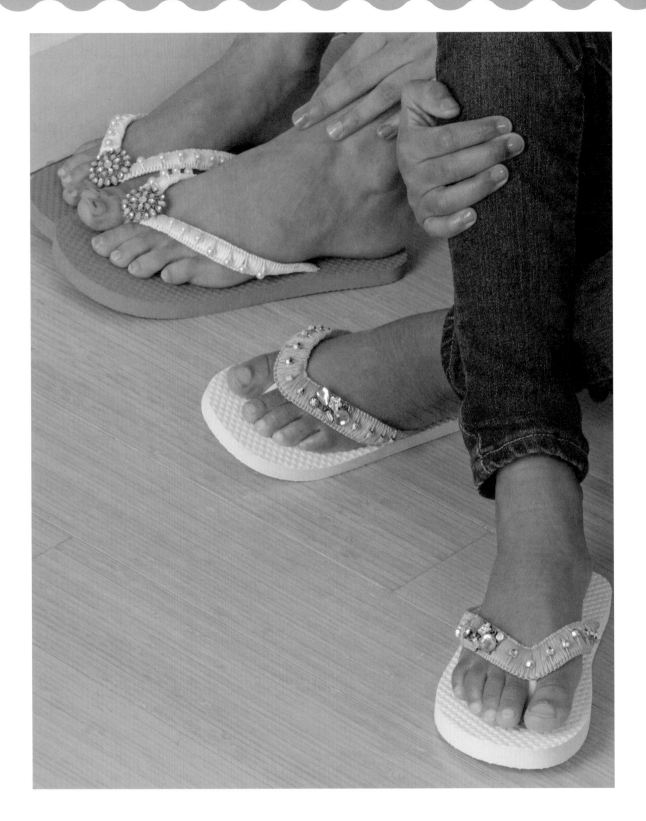

Fancy Flip-Flops

Fine nylon cord was used to cover the straps of these flip-flops to provide a soft look and feel. For a funky, casual design use a thicker nylon cord instead, which would reduce the length of cord needed. Thick cord will also save you some time if you want to whip up a pair in a hurry. Decorate the finished sandals with beads, jewels, or broken jewelry pieces to make them one of a kind!

You will need

- 20 to 24 yards (18 to 22 m) nylon cord (10 to 12 yards [9 to 11 m] per sandal; use a shorter length if using a thicker cord)

- 1 pair flip-flops

- beads with holes large enough to fit over cord

- jewelry decoration to attach to each flip-flop

- small bent wire (optional)

- binder clip (optional)

- thread melting tool

- gem or fabric glue and toothpick

HINT: Since nylon cord is available in various thicknesses, it is helpful to gauge how much cord you will need. Measure and cut a small piece of cord and then knot it over a small section of one of the flip-flop straps. Take the measurement of the covered section and multiply it by the length of the strap to determine how much cord you will need. Add at least 12 extra inches (30.5 cm) to leave you enough extra in case you need it.

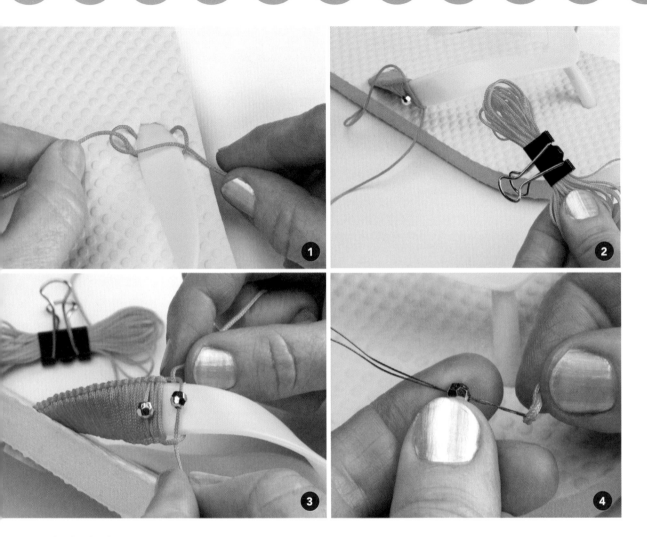

DIRECTIONS

1 Cut a piece of nylon cord 11 to 12 yards (10 to 10.8 m) in length for one flip-flop. Find the middle of the cord and loop it around the base of the strap of the flip-flop.

2 You can wind and bundle the cords and clip each as shown. This will help keep the cords from tangling as you work.

3 Tie a series of square knots (see page 54) over the strap of the sandal. The strap will serve as the core. Add beads as you go along to decorate the sandal.

4 A small bent wire makes it easier to thread the beads over the cord.

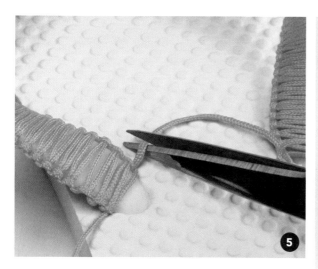

5 Space the beads along the sandal, allowing space for other decorations to be glued on later. When the strap is completely covered, clip off the excess cord and seal the cut ends with a thread melting tool. Complete the other sandal.

6 Use gem or fabric glue to attach jewelry decorations to embellish the flip-flops for extra flare.

Dog Leash

Since paracord is made of nylon, it's the perfect material for making your own sturdy dog leash. Choose two contrasting colors to braid and then add a third color for the handle. This design features a four-strand braid where the colors spiral down the length of the leash. This is an easy project that will have you off and running with your dog in no time!

You will need

- 16-foot (4.9 m) package blue paracord
- 16-foot (4.9 m) package white paracord
- 2 feet (61 cm) camouflage paracord
- spring clip
- thread melting tool

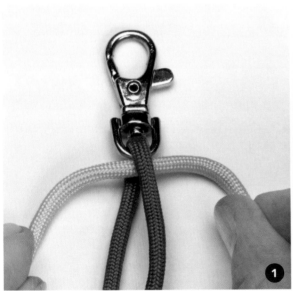

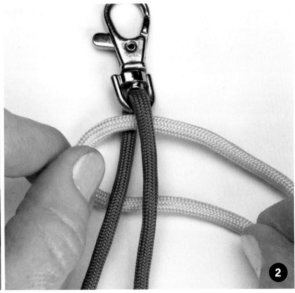

DIRECTIONS

1 Measure to the center of the blue and white cord lengths. Fold the cords at this point and thread the blue one through the spring clip to center the cord on the clip. Place the fold of the white cord under the blue cord as shown.

2 The leash is woven with a four-strand braid as shown opposite. To begin the braid, bring the white cord on the left under the blue cords in the center.

(continued)

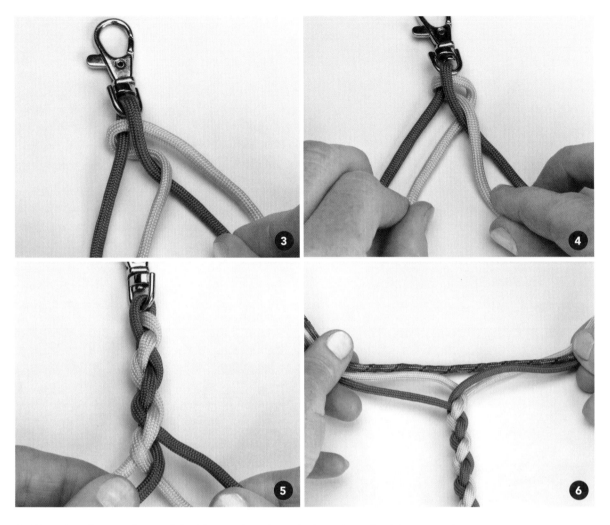

3   Wrap the white cord around the blue cord on the right, bringing it back between the two blue cords.

4   Next, bring the white cord from the right side behind the white and blue cords in the middle. The same white cord then falls between those two cords.

5   Move back to the left side and bring the blue cord behind the middle two cords and back around to the center of the cords and so forth. Move from the left to right side, always wrapping the outside cord behind the middle two and then between, following this pattern to create a braid.

6   Continue braiding the length of the leash. When you are about 12 inches (30.5 cm) from the end you can make a loop handle. Split the braid into two sections with two cords on each side. Place a third cord (camouflage color) along the length of the split cords.

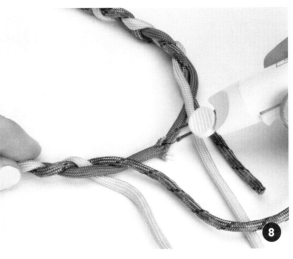

7 Braid the camouflage cord with the other two cords along each side with a three-strand braid as shown on page 50.

8 When you have braided the camouflage along the length of the split cords you can join the ends. Trim the cord ends to be even at both ends. Melt one cord at a time with a thread melting tool. Start with one cord and then braid the other cords around it.

9 After you have woven the last cord in, melt and seal the ends with the thread melting tool.

Crochet

Few things in life are more satisfying than the opportunity to pass on a beloved craft to a younger generation. The connection that develops between the parent, grandparent, or other "grown-up friend" and the child is immense, nurturing a sense of self-esteem, creativity, problem-solving skills, and initiative in the child. The shared memories of crafting together are priceless and last a lifetime.

Over the years, I have taught crochet to my own children, both boys and girls, and more recently, my grandchildren. I have also taught nearly two hundred other children in scout troops, residential summer camps, and community centers. A few "dos" and "don'ts" have emerged, from both the struggles and the successes.

Learning a new craft or skill, can be hard work, but the element of fun—of interest and excitement—needs to be present at all times. Always keep the emphasis on following the interest and commitment level of the child, and the child's attention span, and avoid establishing an "agenda" to achieve a certain amount in a given time period. The bag of crochet supplies can be brought out as an antidote for boredom on a long plane or car ride, when one is recovering from illness, or other times when a physically quiet activity is needed. But when interest flags or the child seems tired, it's time to put it away and do something else. The element of fun is much more important than finishing a certain portion of the project. One small project may take an entire month to complete, but the fun keeps the child coming back for more.

The younger the child, the more important it is to take it slowly. When adults learn a new skill, it's frequently because there is a product or goal in mind. Adults are usually motivated to gain the knowledge as quickly as possible, in order to reach the goal. Children, on the other hand, learn best and enjoy learning the most when they have plenty of time to explore the various aspects and applications of each part of the whole process. Children usually enjoy making multiples of items they've learned to make. They also love to come up with their own variations—after the friendship bracelets (see page 98), they may want (still using only chains) to make longer versions to use as hair wraps, belts, gift-wrap "ribbons," shoe laces, etc. The same dynamic will come into play when they master each new stitch. Don't pressure a child to move on to the next step until he or she is actually in danger of becoming bored with the current skill level. Never cut short the enjoyment of one skill gained, in a hurry to move on to the next lesson or adult-directed project!

Beginners make mistakes, plain and simple. While the pursuit of excellence is a good thing, constant correction feels like criticism and kills the joy of learning. It is important for the actual motions of the hand and direction the yarn moves to be correct—but regularity in the size and shape of the resulting stitches will only come with ractice. A child's joy and pride in his newly made bracelet will NOT be tarnished by the fact that some of the stitches are large and loose while others are tight and small! Muscle memory is gained through repetition of the movement, and as muscle memory grows, the movements themselves become more fluid, more consistent, and more controlled. Projects such as the friendship bracelet, have been designed to be functional and fun, even with highly uneven and "clumsy" stitching. If the child expresses frustration or asks how to correct a mistake,

by all means, jump in and help out. But be sure to point out the positive aspects every time a correction is made.

Children tend to approach a new skill with feverish enthusiasm—for a few days or weeks. When that project or hobby is laid aside in favor of a new adventure, it's easy to believe that the (now languishing) project was a total waste. However, while the child's mind is occupied with other things, quite often their unconscious mind is busily working to move the new knowledge from short-term to long-term memory. This process of mentally "looking away" and refusing to take in more "new" until it's properly internalized is actually a function of real, permanent learning. It's great to take a good long drink at the fountain of knowledge or skill, but the child also needs time to swallow, and to become thirsty again. Keep sessions short; offer a reminder that crochet is a possibility when the child is bored or lacks an activity, but avoid nagging. My own grandmother taught me a few crochet basics, and then I worked (sometimes more "off" than "on") for six years, making enough squares for a blanket. Even in the years when my total crochet output was four successful granny squares plus two or three failed ones, I associated the act of crocheting with the fun I had enjoyed with Nannie. Eventually the yarn was all used up—the 144 squares were made and crocheted together. By the time I graduated high school, the finished blanket became a gift for my mother and a seed of my own lifelong passion for playing with yarn.

—Deborah Burger

Materials and Tools

One of the great things about crochet is that only a few tools are needed, and once gathered, they are quite easy to carry anywhere, either in a zippered plastic bag, a small fabric bag, or a plastic case with a snap closure. You might not use all the materials and tools pictured here in the projects that follow, but they are handy to know about for future projects.

Bates/inline hook (left), Boye/tapered hook (right).

tip If possible, you may want to try a single hook of each shape for the first project, and then decide on a set.

Hooks

First, you'll need a variety of crochet hooks because different sized hooks are needed for different projects. The size of the hook in relation to the size of the yarn being used creates different kinds of fabric—stiff and tight for holding in the stuffing of a toy, or soft and loose for a scarf or blanket. Most craft stores sell hooks either singly or in sets. For the projects in this book, a set that includes sizes F, G, H, I, J, and K will be adequate.

Crochet hooks are made in two different basic shapes, inline and tapered, and most crocheters find that their hands work best with one shape or the other.

Knowing the names of the parts of a crochet hook will make it easier to understand the directions in this book.

In addition to hooks, you'll need a few other tools, including a small scissors, ruler or tape measure, large-eyed yarn needle, sticky notes, and stitch markers.

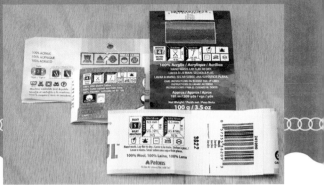

While the beautiful color of a ball of yarn may be the thing that draws your attention, be sure to check the weight symbol before buying it for a specific project!

tip Many items can be used in place of purchased stitch markers—paper clips, bobby pins, or stray "lobster claw" earrings work well. A stitch marker simply needs to be some-thing that can be easily inserted into a stitch, removed when no longer needed there, and is unlikely to fall out on its own.

Most of the projects in this section will use [#4], medium, or "worsted" weight yarn, which is easy to find in craft and department stores. Some of the projects need to be made using a yarn made from cotton (because of the way it absorbs water); some require wool (because of the way it can become solid felt); but most will use acrylic or acrylic blend yarns. Acrylic is a man-made fiber that is easy to wash and dry, and inexpensive to buy. Check each pattern to determine whether you need a specific kind of yarn, or if any yarn of the correct weight will do.

Yarn (and other materials)

It's possible to crochet with any material that can be wrapped around the hook. But most crochet, like most of the projects in this section, is done with yarn. Yarn can be made from many different kinds of fiber, each with its own characteristics. Some are softer or stronger or more absorbent than others. Some can be thrown in the washer and dryer, and others cannot. Some are more stretchy, less scratchy, or more expensive. There seems to be an endless variety of different kinds of yarn. Yarn also comes in different sizes or "weights," such as sock weight or sport weight, just to name a couple. It's important to make sure that the yarn you choose for a project is the same weight as the yarn called for in the pattern, because the size of the yarn determines the size of each stitch, and the size of each stitch determines the size of the finished object. It would be disappointing to end up with a hat that fits a doll when the pattern was for a hat to fit your brother! Most yarn labels have a Yarn Weight Symbol—a little picture of a yarn ball, with a number from 0–6 at the center. Those numbers show the weight of the yarn.

Read the labels carefully to make sure the yarn you choose will work for the project you're making.

Abbreviations

Here is the list of standard abbreviations used for crochet.

approx	approximately
beg	begin/beginning
bet	between
BL	back loop(s)
bo	bobble
BP	back post
BPdc	back post double crochet
BPsc	back post single crochet
BPtr	back post triple crochet
CC	contrasting color
ch	chain
ch-	refers to chain or space previously made, e.g., ch-1 space
ch lp	chain loop
ch-sp	chain space
CL	cluster(s)
cm	centimeter(s)
cont	continue
dc	double crochet
dc2tog	double crochet 2 stitches together
dec	decrease/decreases/decreasing
dtr	double treble
FL	front loop(s)
foll	follow/follows/following
FP	front post
FPdc	front post double crochet
FPsc	front post single crochet
FPtr	front post triple crochet
g	gram(s)
hdc	half double crochet
inc	increase/increases/increasing
lp(s)	loop(s)
Lsc	long single crochet
m	meter(s)
MC	main color
mm	millimeter(s)
MM	move marker

oz	ounce(s)
p	picot
patt	pattern
pc	popcorn
PM	place marker
prev	previous
qutr	quadruple triple crochet
rem	remain/remaining
rep	repeat(s)
rev sc	reverse single crochet
rnd(s)	round(s)
RS	right side(s)
sc	single crochet
sc2tog	single crochet 2 stitches together
sk	skip
Sl st	slip stitch
sp(s)	space(s)
st(s)	stitch(es)
tbl	through back loop(s)
tch	turning chain
tfl	through front loop(s)
tog	together
tr	triple crochet
trtr	triple treble crochet
tr2tog	triple crochet 2 together
WS	wrong side(s)
yd	yard(s)
yo	yarn over
yoh	yarn over hook
[ ]	Work instructions within brackets as many times as directed.
*	Repeat instructions following the single asterisk as directed.
* *	Repeat instructions between asterisks as many times as directed or repeat from a given set of instructions.

Stitch Symbol Key

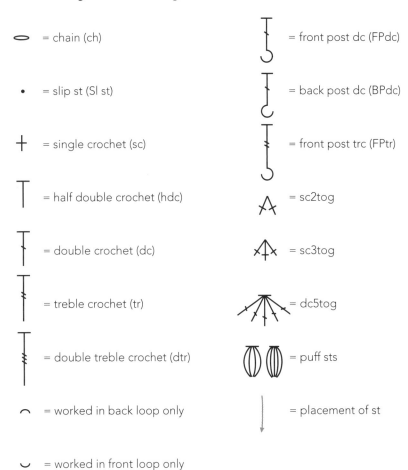

= chain (ch)

= slip st (Sl st)

= single crochet (sc)

= half double crochet (hdc)

= double crochet (dc)

= treble crochet (tr)

= double treble crochet (dtr)

= worked in back loop only

= worked in front loop only

= front post dc (FPdc)

= back post dc (BPdc)

= front post trc (FPtr)

= sc2tog

= sc3tog

= dc5tog

= puff sts

= placement of st

Term Conversions Crochet techniques are the same universally, and everyone uses the same terms. However, US patterns and UK patterns are different because the terms denote different stitches. Here is a conversion chart to explain the differences.

US	UK
single crochet	double crochet
half double crochet	half treble crochet
double crochet	treble crochet
triple crochet	double treble crochet

Stitch Symbol Charts

The limitation to reading worded patterns is that many wonderful projects are designed by people who don't speak the same language! Luckily, crochet also has a universal "picture language," which is understood by crocheters all over the world. Each stitch has a symbol, and the symbols are drawn or printed in order, creating a diagram or picture of the pattern stitch, motif, or whole project.

Reading Symbol Charts in Rows

Symbol charts for a pattern stitch or a whole project made in rows always start at the bottom and on the left side, just opposite of how we read! But think of how a house sits on its foundation. It makes sense to start a piece of crochet with a foundation at the bottom and work upward.

crochet language

Here are the symbols for all the crochet stitches in this section. See page 79 for a full table of standard crochet stitch symbols.

⌐ = chain (ch)

• = slip stitch (sl st)

+ = single crochet (sc)

⊤ = double crochet (dc)

Since crochet projects start with a Foundation Chain, the first step in reading a chart is to locate the row of linked chain symbols at the bottom of the chart and count the number of chains. Turning chains will be shown stacked on top of one another. The line of red ovals (chain stitches) of this chart shows the Foundation of the Crunch Stitch Swatch in this chapter. It shows that the turning chain has been made and Row 1 is about to begin.

Count the 15 chain symbols (in red) and notice that one of them is standing up at the right side—this is the turning chain.

Row 1 is read "backwards," starting at the right hand side, the same direction the hook moves across the row of crochet. Some diagrams provide an arrow to show the direction for each row, but when there is no arrow, look for the turning chain and the row number and start reading the row from there.

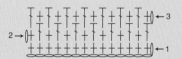

Row 1—in red—starts at the turning chain at the right hand side of the chart.

Row 2 is read from left to right, the "normal" reading direction. Gradually work your way up the chart, reading all the odd numbered rows from right to left (backward) and all the even numbered rows from left to right (frontward).

Try working a new swatch of Crunch Stitch, following the chart instead of the written directions.

Eyelet Directions in Words

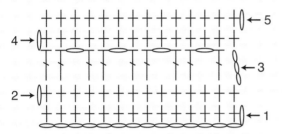

Here's a chart for a pattern using single crochet, double crochet, and chains. Using your practice yarn and hook, try following the chart. If you get confused, use the written directions.

Foundation: Ch 15.

Row 1: Sc in 2nd ch from hook and each ch across. Ch 1, turn.

Row 2: Sc in each st across. Ch 3, turn.

Row 3: Skip first st, dc in next st. *Ch 1, skip next st, dc in each of next 2 sts. Repeat from * across. Ch 1, turn.

Row 4: Sc in each dc, and in each ch-1 space across, ending with sc in top of ch-3 turning chain. Ch 1, turn.

Row 5: Repeat Row 2. Fasten off at end of Row 5.

When a pattern provides both the words and the chart, many crocheters use the two together to figure out parts of the directions that might be confusing.

Reading Charts in the Round

When a project or motif starts at the center and is worked in rounds, like Granny Squares, the chart is also read in the round. Start at the center by locating the chains and the slip stitch that joins the circle. The following chart will make a small flower. You can make the flower from any practice yarn and sew it on as a decoration.

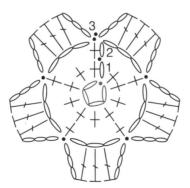

The chain ring is shown in red at the center of the chart.

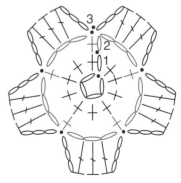

Here's the whole flower chart. Notice that round 3 begins with a longer chain than the earlier rounds.

Techniques

The Slip Knot

To begin, the yarn must be attached to the hook with a loop, and a slip knot works best. Then we will make more loops by pulling yarn through the original one—these are called chains. All crochet projects begin with a slip knot on the hook, and then one or more chain stitches. It's the basic foundation, and a great place to start. If you can tie a bow in your shoelaces, you can tie a slip knot!

You Will Need

Yarn

- medium yarn, of any fiber type

Tools

- hook size J (6 mm)

- scissors

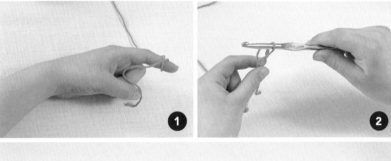

tip Always leave 8–10" (20.5–25.5 cm) of tail (see "crochet language" sidebar) when you make a slip knot. It will come in handy later, and will keep your project from raveling.

1 Make a loop, by crossing the yarn tail over the working yarn. (You can use your finger to help the loop keep its shape.)

2 Push the base of the tail (not the end of the yarn) through the back of the loop you just made. This will form a second loop.

3 Place the hook in the new loop, and pull gently on both yarns to make it snug, but not super tight, on the shaft of the hook.

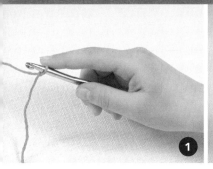 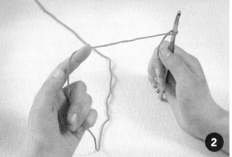 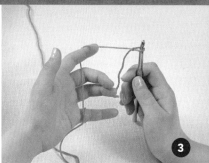

Crochet Language

Working Yarn—the yarn attached to the ball of yarn from which you are working. In crochet, the working yarn is always held at the back of the fabric being created.

Tail—The short length of yarn extending from the slip knot.

Front of the Work—the side closest to you as you crochet.

Back of the Work—the side facing away from you as you crochet.

Right Side—the side of the fabric that will be most viewed (like the outside of a hat or bag) when the project is complete. When working back and forth in rows, the Right Side and Wrong Side will alternately be facing you, and when facing you will be the Front of the Work.

Wrong Side—the side of the fabric that will be less viewed (like the inside of a hat or bag) when the project is complete.

Holding the Hook and Yarn

1 Hold the crochet hook the same way you hold a table knife—with your hand above the hook and your pointer finger at the front, ready to control the loops of yarn on the shaft.

2 The simplest way to hold the yarn is in the fist, with pointer finger held out to move the yarn around the hook. The pinkie and ring fingers curl more or less, to control the tension of the yarn's flow.

3 The looped tension hold makes it easier to control the yarn without tiring the hands. Loop the yarn around the pinkie, then across the palm, and around the tip of the pointer finger.

As you crochet more and more, you'll develop your own way of holding the yarn, and your hands will get less tired, making it easier to create even stitching. Just remember to keep the working yarn over the pointer finger, and keep it about 1" (2.5 cm) from the tip of the hook.

Don't worry if you have to drop and re-position the yarn often, at first. It's a new skill and takes time! Hand muscles will gradually learn and become comfortable with crochet, and it will get easier with practice.

tip Since crochet uses both hands, most left-handed crocheters can hold the hook in their right hand and yarn in the left, just like right-handed crocheters. Each hand has a job to do, and, as with using a keyboard or game controller, one is not easier than the other. Everyone feels a bit awkward in the beginning, whether they are right- or left-handed. One advantage of learning with the hook in the right hand is that you won't have to reverse pattern directions in your head. Right-handed crocheters will find it a bit easier to move the hook, and "lefties" will find it easier to manage the yarn tension and movement.

The Chain Stitch

Most crochet projects begin with a line of linked loops called a Foundation Chain. Chain stitches are also used to create thin lines between solid groups of other stitches and to create open spaces into which other stitches can be worked. Your first project will be made entirely of chains, so let's get started!

1 Make a slip knot and place it on the hook, with the tail closest to you and the working yarn (see "Crochet Language" page 80) away from you. Hold the hook with your pointer finger on the loop of the slip knot, so that it doesn't twirl around the hook. Make sure the chin of the hook is facing toward you.

2 With the pointer finger of your left hand, bring the working yarn up over the top of the hook, and down across the throat of the hook, between the loop already there and the hook's chin. Use your thumb and second finger to pull down gently on the slip knot.

tip Step 2 is called working a "yarn over," although you could just as easily think of it as a "hook under," because the correct way to catch the yarn is for the yarn to move over the hook—keeping the hook under the yarn! This step is part of every crochet stitch, and it's important to get in the habit of doing it in the correct direction to avoid twisting the stitches. In pattern directions, the abbreviation for yarn over is "yo."

3 Turn the chin of the hook to face downward, catching the working yarn under the chin of the hook. Lift the finger holding the slip knot loop, and pull the hook through that loop. Be careful not to allow the original loop to slide down into the throat and tighten there.

4 Patterns usually begin with an instruction to "chain" a certain number of stitches, using the abbreviation, "ch" for the word "chain." So the direction "Ch15" means "Start with a slip knot on your hook. Make 15 chain stitches, not counting that original loop."

Repeat steps 2 and 3 until the motions seem familiar and become comfortable for your hands. It's not necessary for all your chains to be exactly the same size—when the chain is complete, simply holding the first stitch and the last stitch firmly and giving the chain a tug will usually even them out. But it is very important to resist the temptation to make the chains tight and small—future stitches may need to be worked into these chains, so make them loose enough to allow you to stick the tip of the hook into any loop. When your chain is as long as you like, and your hands feel like they know what they're doing, cut the yarn about 8" (20.5 cm) from your last chain stitch, and use the hook to pull the final tail through that last stitch. Pull gently to tighten it, and your stitches are locked in place. This process is called fastening off.

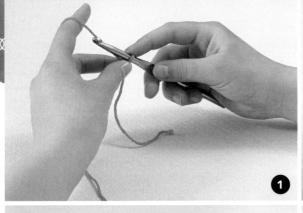

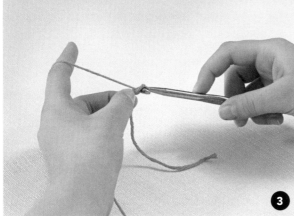

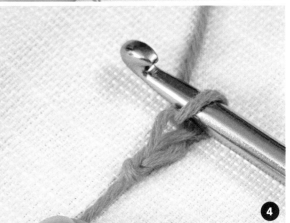

You have created a new loop, the first chain stitch from the slip knot.

1 2 3 4 5 6 7 8 9 10

Ten completed chain stitches.

5 Notice that the little knot at the far left, and the loop still on the hook are not included when counting stitches. Each stitch has a sideways V, made of two strands, on its top. Each stitch also has a third strand, the bottom bump, between and behind the arms of the V.

6 The orange chain at the left shows normal stitches with the right tension—a hook could be poked into any of them. The middle chain is too tight! It looks nice, but will cause frustration later. The chain at the right is very uneven. Holding both ends and tugging may help, but if the stitches can't be counted easily, it won't be easy to work other stitches into them, either.

The Slip Stitch

Chains are great, but they just create straight lines, which will only take you so far. A slip stitch allows you to connect different pieces of any crochet work. The slip stitch is not hard to learn, but since it is your first experience with working into another stitch, it may take some getting used to. As you begin to work into other stitches, you'll see why it is important that you make chains loose enough for the hook to easily poke into an individual chain stitch and pull back through, with a loop of yarn tucked under its chin.

You Will Need

Yarn

- medium, worsted yarn, in any color, 5 yds (4.6 m) or less

Tools

- hook size J (6 mm) or K (6.5 mm)
- scissors

1 Place a slip knot on the hook, and ch 15, loosely (that's pattern language for "make 15 evenly sized chain stitches, large enough for the hook to poke in and out of them easily"). If you look closely at each chain stitch, you'll notice that it's made of three strands of yarn. The top of the stitch is called "sideways V" or "top V" and each of its arms has a name. The strand closest to you is called the front loop, while the strand farther away is called the back loop. These names will be important to know later on, as you make stitches that use the different loops in different ways.

2 At the other end of the chain from the hook, right next to the slip knot and beginning yarn tail, locate the first chain that you made. While holding the working yarn behind the chain, poke the tip of the crochet hook under the two strands of the top V. (See image opposite top.)

3 Keeping the hook below the yarn and the chin of the hook facing you, bring the yarn down across the throat of the hook, and turn the hook's chin downward just a little, to catch the working yarn (yarnover). (See image opposite top.)

4 Pull the yarnover through to the front of the chain, *and* pull it through the loop on the hook. It will take some practice to make this pull through as a single, smooth motion. Don't worry if you need to do it in two steps for now; just remember that in a slip stitch, you must pull the yarnover through *everything*—the stitch you're working into, and the loop on the hook. (See image opposite top.)

Congratulations! Your chain has now become a ring. In a larger project, you might be directed to chain some more or to work other stitches into the ring. For now, fasten off by doing one more yo and pull through the loop on the hook; then cut the yarn 8" (20.5 cm) away and pull the tail through the last loop you made.

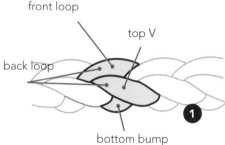

front loop

top V

back loop

bottom bump

Anatomy of a Chain Stitch

Insert the hook under both the front loop and the back loop of the chain stitch.

Facing the hook's chin down allows the hook to pass through the loop, pulling the new loop through.

Pull through to complete the slip stitch.

Slip Stitches in Other Places

Joining stitches with a slip stitch can also be useful at places other than the ends of the chain. A slip stitch can be made into any chain or other crochet stitch. Practice by making a row of chained loops and following the instructions below.

For this practice piece, each instruction is given twice—first using plain English, then in crochet language, which appears in the colored box. Try to follow the crochet language version, but feel free to use the plain English "translation" if you get stuck.

1 Use a slip knot to attach a new piece of yarn to the hook and make twenty-five chain stitches, each large enough that the hook will easily fit into any of them.

2 Skipping the loop on the hook, count ten chains from the hook and make a slip stitch into this chain.

3 Make five chain stitches. Then looking at your Foundation (original base) Chain, slip stitch into the 5th chain from your previous slip stitch, making a little arch or loop with the "new" chain.

4 Repeat step 3 two more times, making the final slip stitch in the very first chain of the Foundation, right next to the original slip knot. Fasten off. You've made four loops along the length of the base chain.

Crochet language

1 Ch 25, loosely.
2 Sl st in 10th ch from hook.
3 Ch 5, skip (or sk) next 4 ch; Sl st in next ch.
Rep Step 3 twice, ending with Sl st in last ch of Foundation. Fasten off—4 loops made.

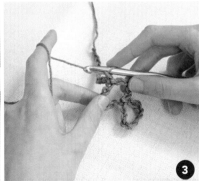

The Single Crochet

When your hands are comfortable making slip stitches, you're ready to learn the single crochet stitch. Single crochet has one more step than a slip stitch, and that extra step gives the stitch actual height. If you think in terms of drawing, the chains you've made so far are like thin lines, and slip stitches are like dots or intersections in the line. Single crochet could be compared to using a "fat line" marker to create much wider lines when drawing. These lines can also be stacked up to make solid fabric, like the strokes of a marker when filling in a shape. First you'll learn to form the stitch; then you'll make a couple of projects that allow you to start each single crochet stitch in an easy-to-find place.

Get Ready

You Will Need

Yarn

- medium yarn, 5 yds (4.6 m) or less

Tools

- hook size J (6 mm) or K (6.5 mm)

Foundation: Ch 8 and join with a Sl st to form ring. Ch 1. (Plain English translation: Make a slip knot and place it on the hook. Make 8 chain stitches and then slip stitch into the first chain to join the two ends into a ring. Now make 1 more chain stitch.)

1 With the working yarn held at the back of the work (that is, on the side facing away from you), poke the tip of the crochet hook into the center of the ring from front to back. In crochet stitches, the hook always goes into the work from front to back, never from back to front.

2 Yarn over (yo) and use the chin of the hook to pull the yarnover back through the ring to the front of the work. There are now 2 loops on the hook.

tip A row or round of crochet stitches other than slip stitch always begins with a "turning chain." The purpose of the turning chain is to raise the height of the work to the height of the stitches in the row about to be made. The turning chain will be made up of one chain stitch if the first "real" stitch is to be single crochet. More chain stitches are needed in turning chains for taller stitches.

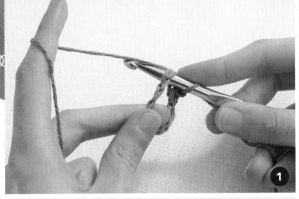

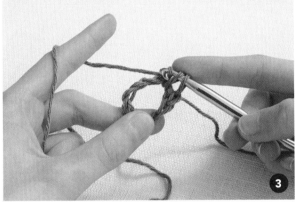

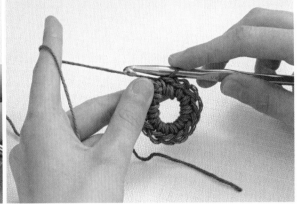

This last step, "yarn over and pull through 2 loops," is the basic building block of crochet. All the plain and all the fancy stitches are built from combinations of yarnovers and pulling through!

Twelve completed single crochets (sc) in the ring.

3 With the hook's chin facing you, yarn over, turn the chin of the hook face down to catch the yarnover, and pull the yarnover through both of the loops on the hook.

Repeat steps 1, 2, and 3 eleven more times. You'll notice that the single crochet (sc) stitches stand next to each other, going around the ring, and that their top Vs look just like chain stitches. As you make more stitches in the ring, be careful not to make a stitch right on top of, or working around, another single crochet you've already made. If the space in the ring begins to seem "used up", and you've made fewer than ten single crochets within it, simply push the finished single crochets to the right. They should slide along the ring, crowding together close to the turning chain, and freeing up more space to work.

Let's take a close look at the single crochet stitch and name the parts of the stitch so that later instructions will be easier to understand. In addition to the labeled parts, there is a right leg and a left leg on the back or "wrong side" of the stitch.

tip When "drawing up a loop," you use the hook to "catch" the working yarn at the back of the fabric (the side away from you) and pull that new loop through to the front of the work.

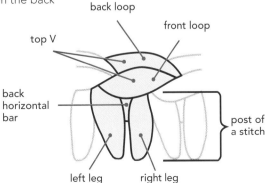

back loop

front loop

top V

back horizontal bar

post of a stitch

left leg

right leg

Chain Foundation for Working in Rows

The chain that starts a row-based project is usually longer than the chains you've started with up until now. Generally, the starting, or Foundation Chain, is as long as the width of the square or rectangle being made. Imagine a winter scarf—if you start with a chain about 6" (15 cm) long and make *many* rows back and forth, you'll eventually end up with a long, narrow rectangle to wrap around your neck. Or, you could start with a very long chain and work a few very long rows to make the same shape. In other words, your rows can go across the short side of the rectangle or the long side. One way is not better than the other, but the two approaches create different looks.

Besides the length of the chain, another difference is in how the chain is used. Instead of making a ring and working the first single crochets into the "hole" at the center of the ring, this time you'll be making the first row of single crochet directly into chain stitches. Here is where it becomes very important to make the Foundation Chain loosely—the hook must go into each chain stitch without a fight. So, let's get going, chaining and rowing!

You Will Need

Yarn

- any worsted yarn in a light color, a few yards or small ball

Tools

- hook size H (5 mm) and I (5.5 mm), or J (6 mm) and K (6.5 mm)

- scissors

- 2 stitch markers

tip Count the stitches at the end of each row (by counting the top Vs), to make sure there are ten. If there are fewer, look for a hole between two stitches, and see if you can find the chain that was skipped. It will be there between the two stitches on either side of it. If you have more than ten, look for a place where the work seems to bend in an "elbow"—that will be where you increased by working two stitches in the same place. If you can find the spot where the mistake happened, carefully pull out the stitches just back to that point, and then finish the row correctly. If you can't easily find the exact mistake spot, simply pull out that row—the marker in the first stitch will prevent you from pulling out too many—and do the row over again.

Many crocheters always make their Foundation Chains with a larger hook than they use for the rest of the rows.

Insert the hook under 2 strands of the 2nd chain from hook. It's easiest to put the hook under the back loop and bottom bump.

Complete the sc stitch as usual: yo and pull through both loops on the hook. The first single crochet into the chain is complete. Place a stitch marker in the top of this stitch.

Look for the very next chain loop to the left of the stitch just completed. Be careful not to skip a chain.

Finished row of 10 single crochet. Stitch marker shows the first st in the row.

1 STARTING CHAIN AND FIRST ROW

Foundation: With the larger of the two hooks, chain eleven loosely. Count the chains to double check, and then switch to the smaller hook.

Look closely at the chain you've just made. The loop on the hook does not get counted. The next loop below the hook is the "first ch from the hook" and is also the "turning chain" for a single crochet row. You will not work into it. The next chain beyond that is the "2nd ch from hook" and pattern instructions will tell you to insert the hook into it.

Continue across the chain, making 1 sc in each ch st.

Make 1 chain stitch, the "turning chain."

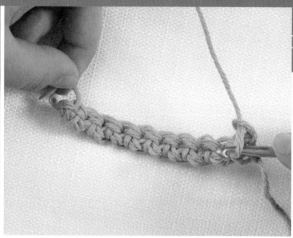

Turn the work, just like turning the page of a book. Now the stitch marker is at the other end, because the first stitch of Row 1 will be the last stitch you'll work into in Row 2.

Insert the hook here to start the first stitch of Row 2 and work a single crochet. When the first stitch is finished, place a stitch marker in the top of it.

Locating the final stitch of the row—look for the stitch marker and make the last stitch of Row 2 in the marked stitch. As soon as you find it, you can remove the stitch marker to make it easier to insert the hook.

Row 2 is finished! The marker at the right hand edge will help in working the final stitch of Row 3.

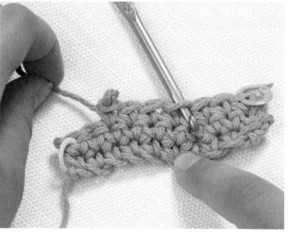

Using the hook as a guide in "frogging" to fix a mistake.

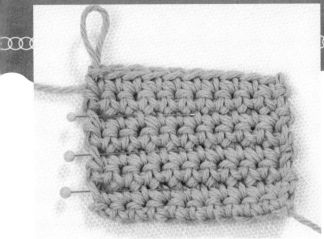

The pins are placed every two rows, to show how rows of single crochet are counted by "twosies."

Making the Turn

When crocheting in rows, each new row begins with a "turning chain." Some patterns will say to turn the work and then make the chain as you begin the next row; others will tell you to make the turning chain and then turn the work. The order in which you do these steps doesn't matter; some designers just prefer to write it one way or the other. What *is* important is that you always remember to turn the work and to make the turning chain the correct length.

The length of the turning chain depends on what stitch is being done in the *next* row. The turning chain must include enough chain stitches to equal the height of the stitches in the new row. A single crochet stitch is 1 chain stitch high, but there are other, taller stitches to learn later, and they will have longer turning chains—2, 3, or 4 ch stitches!

Onward and Upward— Row 2 and Beyond

Begin Row 2 by locating the first stitch. There is a loop on the hook; just below that is the turning chain, and the next loop is the top V of the first stitch of the row.

Now work a single crochet stitch in each stitch across the row. Remember to insert the hook under both the front loop and the back loop (under both arms of the sideways V) at the top of each stitch.

It's important to count stitches at the end of every row until your eyes get used to the look of the fabric. Counting stitches is the best way to figure out if you accidentally made two stitches in the same place (added a stitch) or accidentally skipped a stitch, leaving a little hole in the work (lost a stitch). If either has happened, insert the hook between the two top loops at the top of the last correct stitch before the mistake and then gently rip out stitches until you reach the error. The placement of the hook will ensure that you don't rip out too many.

Work several more rows, remembering to make a turning chain between the end of one row and the beginning of the next, using the two stitch markers to keep track of the final stitch in each row. You'll notice that the fabric has a different texture than the fabric that was made by working single crochet in rounds! When worked in rounds, as in the hat and bag, each round created one ridge or bump in the fabric. Now, working in rows, the ridges or bumps are more gentle, and it takes two rows to make each little "furrow." It's easy to count by twos when counting rows of single crochet.

When you're comfortable with crocheting in rows, you're ready for the projects that follow. Each of these projects will use the skills you already know, and also teach something new.

Making the Double Crochet Stitch

Here you'll learn how to make the most commonly used taller stitch: the double crochet, or dc. You'll work the stitch in both rounds and rows to create a soft and warm winter scarf, the Great Grannies Scarf (see page 108). Find some yarn to practice—leftovers from earlier projects will be fine—and choose a hook large enough to allow you to easily make the stitches you already know with your practice yarn.

You Will Need

Yarn

- worsted (medium) weight of any fiber, 2 colors

Tools

- hook size H (5 mm), I (5.5 mm), or J (6 mm)
- 1 stitch marker

1 GET READY

Starting with a chain ring is familiar and works as well for double crochet as single crochet.

Foundation: Ch 6. Join with a sl st to form a ring. Ch 3.

Taller Stitch = Longer Turning Chain

The purpose of the turning chain is to create the height of the stitches in the new row that is about to be crocheted. Since the double crochet stitch is as tall as three chains, every round or row of dc starts with three chains. The turning chain actually counts as a double crochet stitch—the first stitch of each round or row. However, it doesn't look exactly like a dc stitch, and it's easy to accidentally skip working into it in the following round or row. To help with this, place a stitch marker in the top (3rd) ch of the turning chain.

2 BEGIN THE DC WITH A YARN OVER

Before inserting the hook into the ring, yarn over, and use your pointer finger to hold the yarn over with the loop already on the hook.

3 INSERT AND DRAW UP

Stick the hook into the ring as you would to sc, still holding the yarn over and the original loop on the hook with your index finger. At the back of the work, yarn over as you would for sc, then draw that loop back through to the front of the work, just as you would for sc.

4 WORK TWO LOOPS OFF THE HOOK

Yarn over and pull through two loops, leaving two loops on the hook.

5 WORK THE LAST TWO LOOPS OFF THE HOOK

Yarn over again and pull through two loops.

Congratulations! You've made a double crochet! Repeat steps 2–5 ten more times. Join with a Sl st in the top (marked) ch of the beginning ch-3. Fasten off with a final locking chain, and pull the tail through that loop. Dc stitches can be counted by their top Vs (like sc) or by their vertical posts. The top V is slightly to the right of the post when looking at the right side of the work.

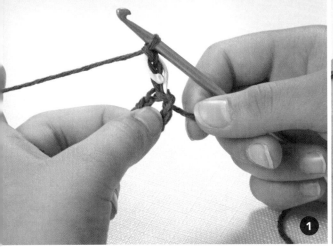

A stitch marker in the top of the turning chain makes it easier to find later. The turning chain counts as the first stitch of the round.

Make sure the working yarn is held at the back of the work, under the hook.

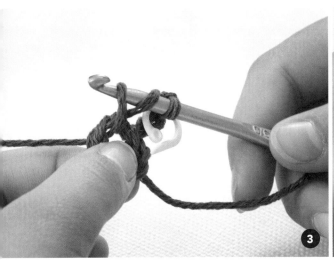

There are now three loops on the hook.

Dc stitch, halfway finished.

Completed double crochet stitch, standing next to the beginning ch-3.

There are now 12 dc in the ring—the marked ch-3 to start, the first stitch, and the ten repeats.

Going On with Rounds or Rows

Attaching New Yarn with a Double Crochet

In making many motifs the pattern depends on changing the color of yarn used for each round. One traditional way to attach the new color is to place a slip knot on the hook, slip stitch into the correct place and then ch 3 to start the dc round. But this method leaves a visible knot at the soft base of the stitches. Instead, attach the new yarn color with a double crochet!

1 YARN OVER

With a slip knot of the new color on the hook, yarn over, using your pointer finger to hold the yarn over and the starting loop together firmly. Make sure the working yarn passes beneath the hook and is held at the back of the piece to which you're attaching it.

2 INSERT THE HOOK

While still holding the two loops on the hook, find the correct place (according to pattern directions) to insert the hook. In this case, with RS facing, insert the hook into any of the dc stitches of the finished round, making sure to go under both loops of the top V.

3 COMPLETE THE DC STITCH AS USUAL

Yarn over, then draw the loop to the front of the work and up to the height of the new stitch. Yarn over and pull through two loops; yarn over and draw through the two remaining loops.

It's not ideal to have a knot at the soft base of the next round of double crochet!

Ready to insert the hook into the top of a stitch.

The slip knot is now in a position where it will be much easier to hide inside another stitch when weaving in the yarn tails.

The left swatch shows the first stitch of each row correctly skipped. The center swatch shows an increase in each row caused by *not* skipping the first stitch. And the right swatch shows the result of forgetting to work a row's last stitch into the top of the turning chain, losing 1 stitch per row.

One More "Tricky Bit"— the Turning Chain, in Rows

Starting a New Row

When working with double crochet stitches in rounds, a stitch marker helps to locate the top of the beginning ch-3. The joining slip stitch goes into that marked chain, and if the color isn't being changed, the next round begins with a new ch-3, with its top ch marked, which counts as the first dc of the round.

When working dc sts back and forth in rows, that "ch 3 to turn and start the new row" also counts as the first stitch in the row. Until you become comfortable with locating it, it's important to always mark the top of the turning chain and to skip the first stitch of the row—the turning chain will not be standing exactly in the top of the end stitch, but you must count it as if it were. The turning chain counts as the stitch in that first space. If you also make a double crochet in that stitch, you will have increased, just as if you worked two stitches in the same place.

Braided Chains Friendship Bracelet

Here's a fun way to use crocheted chains! If you make one for yourself, you'll need a friend to measure your wrist. If you're making a bracelet for a friend, you can do the measuring. The possible color combinations are endless, so you can make these bracelets in each person's favorite colors, in school or club colors, or in seasonal and holiday colors. It's also fun to use a mix of solid colors and variegated yarn.

You Will Need

Yarn

- medium (worsted) cotton yarn, such as Lily Sugar 'n Cream or Knit Picks Dishie, 5 yds (4.6 m) each of 3 colors

Size

- Any size for any wrist!

Tools

- any size hook comfortable for use. [Sample was made with a G (4.25 mm) hook.]
- scissors
- tape measure or ruler
- friend

tip For the projects in this book, the Key Measurement is like a target. You'll need to measure carefully and then follow the directions to crochet until your crocheted piece reaches the Key Measurement. Not every project has a Key Measurement, but when there is one, it's important to pay attention to it so that your project will fit properly.

Directions

1 Measure the wrist of the person who will be wearing the bracelet. Add 1" (2.5 cm) and write down the total, which is the Key Measurement for this project.

2 With the first color yarn, leave a 10" (25.5 cm) tail and place a slip knot on the hook. Make as many chains as needed to reach the Key Measurement when the chain is laid flat and not stretched. Make the chain stitches as even in size as possible. Cut the yarn 10" (25.5 cm) from the last stitch, and fasten off by pulling the tail through the final chain. Repeat step 2 with each of the colors of yarn.

3 Tie the three beginning tail strands together just below the slip knots with an overhand knot. Have a friend hold the knot or secure the knot by pinning it to something solid. Braid the three chains together. Tie the ending tails together after the final chains with another overhand knot.

4 About an inch from the outer end of each set of tails, tie them together with another overhand knot and trim the ends to the same length. Use these ties to tie the bracelet to your friend's wrist.

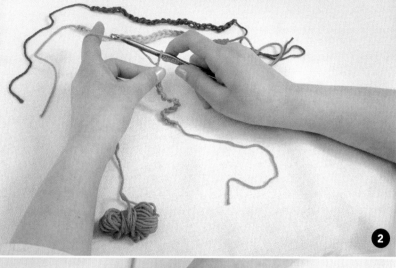

tip More project fun! You can make a headband using this same technique. Measure your head, or your friend's head, and add 2" (5 cm) for your Key Measurement. Ankle bracelets can be made adding 1" (2.5 cm) to the ankle measurement. Belts, like headbands, will need 2" (5 cm) added to the waist measurement.

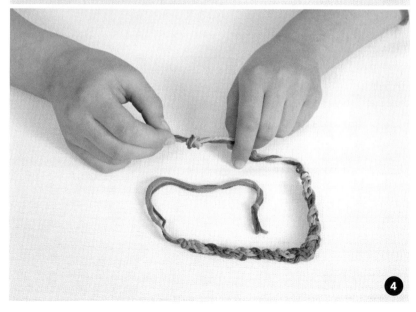

Monster Madness!

With yarn and a bit of fluff for stuffing, you can make an endless variety of stuffed "critters" for yourself, brothers and sisters, and your friends. If you choose different colors of yarn, and felt or sewn features, each one you make will be different and special, whether cute and cuddly or "too ugly not to love."

You Will Need

Yarn

- worsted (medium) acrylic or wool blend, 100 yds (91.4 m) or less of color A, about 25 yds (22.9 m) of color B and scraps of black and any other desired colors for face embroidery. (Sample was made with Red Heart Soft.)

Tools

- hook size G (4 mm) and I (5.5 mm)
- scissors
- 2 stitch markers
- yarn needle
- polyester fiberfill stuffing
- 2 or more small buttons
- sewing thread and thread needle
- scraps of colored craft felt for face, optional

Stitches and Abbreviations

ch—chain

Sl st—slip stitch

sc—single crochet

st(s)—stitch(es)

RS—right side

WS—wrong side

Gauge

7 stitches = 2" (5 cm), 7 rows = 2" (5 cm)

Gauge is not crucial for this project, but use a hook that makes a fairly tight fabric so the stuffing will not peek out between stitches.

Directions

Note: Numbers at the end of a line of directions indicate the number of stitches in that row. If no number is given, the stitch count is the same as it was in the row before.

1 CROCHET MAIN PIECE (HEAD AND BODY)

Foundation: With color A and smaller hook, ch 16 loosely. (Use a larger hook if your chains tend to be tight.)

Row 1: Sc in 2nd ch from hook and place marker if needed. Sc in each ch across. Ch 1, turn—15 sc.

Rows 2–36: Sc in each st across. Ch 1, turn. At end of Row 36, fasten off.

2 ASSEMBLE MAIN PIECE

Using color A yarn, start the seam at the left hand side where Row 36 meets the Foundation Chain. Make 1 sc in each row end, working through both thicknesses, toward the fold. This will join Row 36 to Row 1, Row 35 to Row 2, etc. At fold, fasten off—18 sc.

Attach a new color A yarn to the hook. At the opposite edge of the fold, sc through both thicknesses to close the other long side, making 1 sc in each row end, and continuing to keep rows straight and matched. Fasten off.

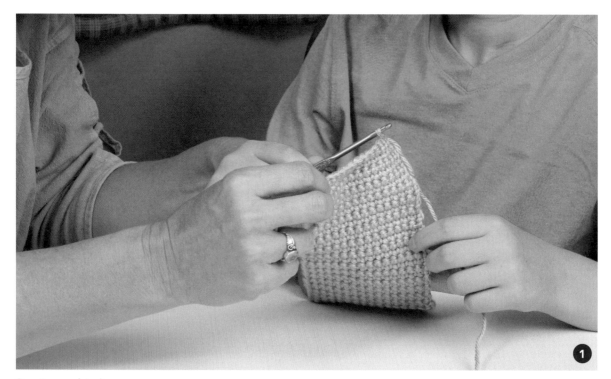

Step 1, completed.

Starting the second seam by attaching the yarn on the hook to the work with a single crochet stitch.

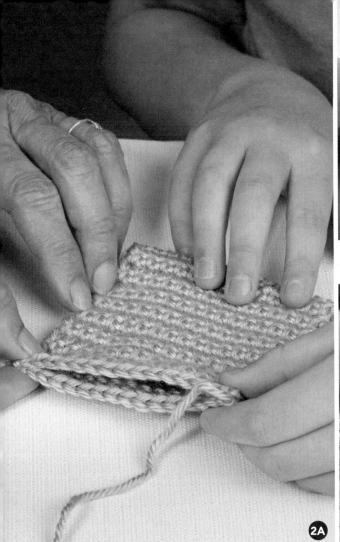

Fold the rectangle in half widthwise so that the Foundation Chain and Row 36 are together.

Markers placed for ears.

3 MAKE THE EARS

Hold the Main Piece so that the folded edge is at the top and the open edge is at the bottom. *On right-hand edge, count down five rows from fold and place a marker in the seam. Count five stitches across the fold from the edge and place another marker.

Cut a piece of color A yarn about 18" (45.5 cm) long and thread it onto the yarn needle. Pull half the yarn through to create a double strand. Leaving about 4" (10 cm) of tail sticking out, sew a line of stitches from the first marker to the 2nd marker. Weave in the ending tail and cut it close to the crocheted fabric. Rethread the starting tail onto the needle (you can do the two strands separately if you need to) and weave it in as well. Trim it off close to the crocheted fabric. Repeat from * on left hand side of Main Piece for second ear. *(continued)*

tip If all the ends have been properly fastened off (with a final "yarn over and pull the tail through"), it's easy to simply poke them inside and hide them in the stuffing. To do this, thread a tail onto the yarn needle. Stick the needle into the stuffed piece and through some of the stuffing, then back out 1" or 2" (2.5 cm or 5 cm) away. Cut off the yarn close to the surface. Friction from the stuffing, along with the fastening off, will hold the end securely inside the toy.

4 STUFF THE BODY

Hold the Main Piece with ears at the bottom and the open edge at the top. Add polyester fiberfill stuffing a small amount at a time, tucking it down into the corners gently but firmly, until filled. Less stuffing makes a softer, flatter finished toy; more stuffing makes a fatter, firmer toy.

When stuffed, attach color A yarn to hook and sc through the thicknesses of both the Foundation Chain and Row 36 to close the seam. Fasten off—15 sc.

Now weave in any remaining yarn tails on the project so far.

5 MAKE THE LEGS (MAKE 2)

Foundation: With the larger hook and color B, leaving 10–12" (25.5–30.5 cm) tail, ch 11 loosely.

Row 1: 2 sc in 2nd ch from hook, and 2 sc in each ch across. Ch 1, turn—20 sc.

Row 2: 2 sc in each st across. Ch 1, turn—40 sc.

Row 3: 2 sc in each st across. Fasten off, leaving 10–12" (25.5–30.5 cm) of tail—80 sc.

When both legs are finished, use the tails, threaded through the yarn needle, to sew them to the bottom edge of Main Piece near the outside edges, hiding the tails inside the stuffing. Trim tails off close to the surface.

6 MAKE THE ARMS (MAKE 2)

Foundation: With larger hook and color B, ch 8 loosely.

Row 1: 2 sc in 2nd ch from hook. 2 sc in each st across. Ch 1, turn—14 sc.

Row 2: 2 sc in each st. Fasten off, leaving 10–12" (25.5–30.5 cm) tail. Weave in starting tail—28 sc.

Use the ending tails to sew an arm to each side of the body, halfway between the base of an ear and the bottom corner. The ending tail was left longer, so there's enough to sew across the width of the arm a couple of times in different directions, for sturdiness. After sewing back and forth, hide the remaining tail inside the stuffing and trim it off at the surface.

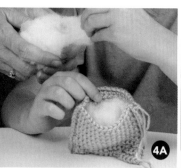

Avoid lumpiness by adding the stuffing little by little.

Pull the edges together around the stuffing, and poke in the stuffing as needed.

Hiding yarn tails in the stuffing.

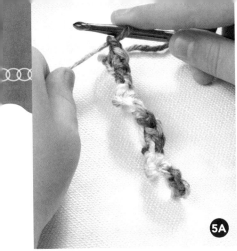

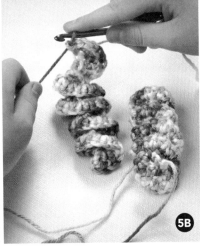

The leg begins to curl with the increases in Row 1.

Two completed legs.

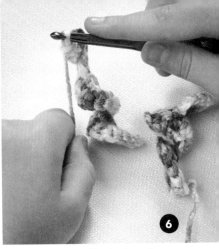

The arms are just like the legs, but smaller and a little less curled.

tips It's best to sew on a leg with one tail and hide that tail inside the stuffing, then sew again with the second tail. This makes a more sturdy connection than a few stitches done at once with both tails doubled in the needle.

If the toy is to be a gift for a small child (3 years or under), safety requires that the face be embroidered with yarn. Babies and toddlers can bite off buttons and swallow them!

7 MAKE A FUN FACE

Use the photo as a guide (or be bold and use your own imagination) to sew on buttons or glue on felt or fabric for the eyes, nose, and mouth. Be creative—who says your critter, monster, or alien must have two eyes? It could have three or one or six! Use yarn to sew on a smile, a nose, or whatever other features in whatever colors you like.

Great Grannies Scarf

You'll get lots of practice with both rounds and rows of dc in this project, a scarf that uses both motifs and solid rows of double crochet. With a pair of Granny Square motifs at each end, this warm and soft scarf is also bright and colorful! The motifs are made separately, attached to each other in pairs, and then the rows of double crochet are worked to connect the two ends.

You Will Need

Yarn

- worsted (medium) any fiber type, in 4 colors: Color A,10–15 yds (9.1–13.7 m); Color B, 20–30 yds (18.3–27.4 m); Color C, 40–50 yds (36.6–45.7 m); Color D, 80–100 yds (73.2–91.4 m)

Tools

- hook size J (6 mm) or K (6.5 mm)
- scissors
- tape measure
- yarn needle
- 2 stitch markers

Stitches and Abbreviations

ch—chain

Sl st—slip stitch

dc—double crochet

st(s)—stitch(es)

sp(s)—space(s)—the large hole created under a ch-1 or ch-2 in the pattern

rnd—round

RS—right side

WS—wrong side

PM—place marker

MM—move marker

( )—Parentheses enclose a group of stitches to be worked in the same stitch or space

Gauge

First round of motif = 2" (5 cm) across; in Scarf pattern, 8 sts and 6 rows = 3" (7.5 cm).

While exact gauge is not important for this project, you may want to experiment with hook size to make sure that the fabric you'll be making is soft and not stiff, but also not so loose that the scarf won't be warm.

tip For any project with more than one color, use the same yarn for all the colors or make sure that the various yarns can be laundered the same way. For example, do not use acrylic yarn for one color and wool yarn for another color. When washed, the wool might shrink while the acrylic will not.

Directions

SUGGESTED GAUGE SWATCH

Making a gauge swatch will help you decide if the size of hook is working well with the chosen yarn. It's also a great opportunity to practice making rows of double crochet. Here's how:

Foundation: Ch 17. Place first marker in last ch made (immediately below the hook).

Row 1: Dc in 4th ch from hook and each ch across. Ch 3, marking top of chain with 2nd marker, turn.

Row 2: Skip first st (turning ch counts as first st). Dc in next st and each st across, including the marked ch of the Foundation. Ch 3, and move the marker to the top of this turning chain. Turn—15 dc, counting turning ch.

Row 3: Repeat Row 2, working into the marked chain from Row 1. Do not fasten off, but pull the final loop out large enough so the work doesn't unravel. Take a look at the swatch. Does it have the thickness, softness, and desirable drape for your scarf? If it seems thick, lumpy, and stiff, use a larger hook for the project. If it seems too loose, droopy, and holey, use a smaller hook for the project.

1 MAKE 4 GRANNY SQUARES

Foundation: With A, ch 4 and join with a Sl st in first ch to form a ring.

Rnd 1: Ch 3 (counts as first dc here and throughout), 2 dc in ring, *ch 2, 3 dc in ring. Repeat from * twice. Ch 2, join with a Sl st in top ch of beginning ch-3. Fasten off—4 groups of 3 dc, 4 ch-2 spaces.

Rnd 2: With RS of Rnd 1 facing, attach B with a dc in any corner ch-2 space. (2 dc, ch 2, 3 dc, ch 1) in same ch-2 sp. * (3 dc, ch 2, 3 dc, ch 1) in next ch-2 sp. Repeat from * twice. Join with a Sl st in top of first dc. Fasten off—4 corners with 2 groups of 3 dc each, 1 ch-1 sp on each side of square.

Rnd 3: With RS facing, attach C with a dc in any corner ch-2 sp. (2 dc, ch 2, 3 dc, ch 1) in same sp. *(3 dc, ch 1) in next ch-1 sp; (3 dc, ch 2, 3 dc, ch 1) in

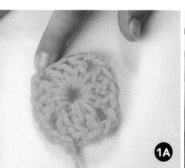

First round is finished and fastened off.

Joining with a slip stitch in the top of the attaching double crochet.

Working a round of single crochet around the square.

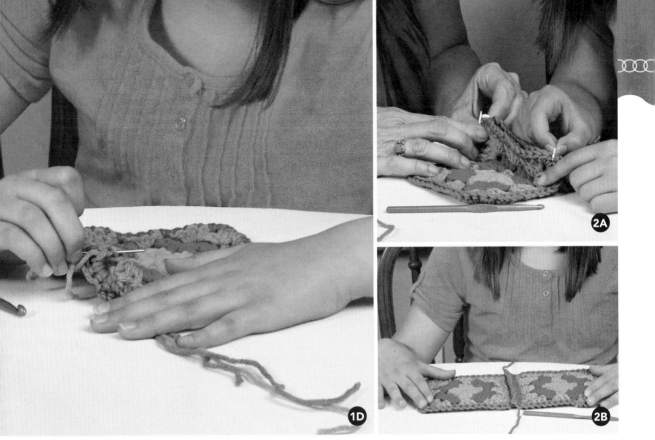

Finished granny square

Paired squares

next corner ch-2 sp. Repeat from * twice; join with a Sl st in first dc. Fasten off—4 corners with 2 groups of 3 dc each, 1 group of 3 dc and 2 ch 1 spaces on each side of square.

Rnd 4: With RS facing, attach D with a sc in any corner ch-2 sp. 2 sc in same space. *Sc in each dc and in each ch-1 sp across to next corner. 3 sc in corner ch-2 sp. Repeat from *twice, sc in each dc and in each ch-1 sp of final side. Join with a Sl st in first sc. Fasten off—3 sc in each corner, 15 sc per side including corner stitches in count.

Weave in yarn tails as soon as you've checked that the square is correct (4 equal sides and 4 equal corners). Make 3 more squares.

2 PAIR THE SQUARES

Hold two squares with WS of each facing. On top edge of both pieces held together, locate the center sc of each corner and pin the two squares together through these two stitches, using stitch markers as pins.

Use color D to single crochet through the edge sts of both granny squares together, from one marker to the other, making sure to match stitches on the two squares.

Attach the other two squares in the same manner, but leave the two pairs separate from each other, as one pair will form each end of the scarf.

(continued)

3 CROCHET THE SCARF IN DC AND SC ROWS

In this step, you'll be alternating rows of dc and sc. This pairing of rows makes a strong and soft fabric, and gives you practice in making the correct turning chain for each height of stitch.

Row 1: Hold one pair of joined grannies with RS facing and one short side of the rectangle upward. Attach color D with a dc in the corner stitch. Dc in each st across to next corner st. Ch 1, turn—15 dc.

Row 2: Sc in each st across. Ch 3, turn. PM in top (3rd) ch of turning ch-3—15 sc.

Row 3: Skip first st, dc in each st across. Ch 1, turn—15 dc.

Row 4: Sc in each st across, including first st and marked ch at end of the row. Ch 3, MM to top of this new turning ch.

Repeat Rows 3 and 4 until the whole piece measures 36" (91.5 cm) or to desired length (remember that the scarf will be lengthened by the pair of grannies yet to be added). Stop after a Row 3 (dc row). Turn as if to start the next Row 4. WS of the first pair of grannies is now facing you. Do not fasten off.

Row 1 finished, with correct turning ch for the next row's height.

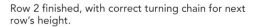

3B

Row 2 finished, with correct turning chain for next row's height.

3C

Second pair of Granny Squares being attached by slip stitch on the wrong side of the scarf. When the final yarn tails are woven in, the scarf will be ready to wear.

4 ATTACH THE FINAL GRANNIES

With WS of scarf facing and holding the hook at the right hand edge, prepare to start the joining row. Lay the remaining pair of grannies end to end with the scarf, WS of scarf facing up. Pick up the scarf and grannies together, with RS touching and WS facing you. Matching stitches of the two pieces and working through both thicknesses, sl st in each st across. Fasten off. Weave in remaining yarn tails.

Granny Square Projects

There are so many things you can make from Granny Squares. Here are a few ideas to get you started:

1 Make a scarf entirely from squares. Make ten or twelve Granny Squares, and attach them to each other in a long line.

2 Make a blanket from one gigantic Granny Square. Use up all your scrap yarn by continuing to make round after round of the double crochet repeat. Save Round 4 for the very end and use it as an edging. Whenever one color of yarn runs out, just add the next color and keep going.

3 Make a blanket from lots of squares. Sixty-four squares made exactly like the ones in the scarf pattern and crocheted together in eight rows

of eight squares with a final round of single crochet, will make a nice-size blanket. This will require about 36 oz (1020 g) of yarn. You can mix up the order in which you use the colors in each square to add visual interest.

4 Make a bag by joining four Granny Squares to each other in a 2 x 2 square for each side. Make a strap by working rows of single crochet or double crochet as wide and long as you like.

5 There are many other square motif patterns in various sizes available in magazines, books, and on the Internet. Any of them can be used in place of the Granny to make any of these items.

Knitting

The art of knitting predates the written word. So while a book about how to do it will be helpful for modern learners, it's not the whole story. The very best way to learn knitting is to do it together with friends and loved ones.

If you are an adult, either teaching or learning together with a child, this section will take you step by step through the basics, and then beyond. If you are a child, either teaching or learning together with an adult, the process should be much the same.

In either case, this section is simple and intuitive. You can choose to read through the process and practice each step. Or you can pick a project you like, and follow the steps for making it. Each pattern will direct you to the information you need.

In addition to projects and techniques, yarn and knitted fabric, the pages that follow will tell you about tools that make knitting easier and more fun, and a few of the many great ways to connect with other knitters.

It is my great privilege to introduce new knitters of all ages to the delights that await you in the world of yarn and needles. The best thing about knitting is the people who do it. Welcome, and thank you for joining us!

I invite you to sit side by side, hold each other's yarn, and discover the magic of playing with string. Together.

—*Mary Scott Huff*

Materials and Tools

What makes knitting so great is that it only requires a few tools that you can take anywhere. You might not use all the materials and tools pictured here in the projects that follow, but they are handy to know about for future projects.

Weight

The first characteristic to compare between the specified yarn and your substitution is its weight. Generally speaking, the heavier the weight, the larger needle you'll use, resulting in fewer and larger stitches in each 1" (2.5 cm) of knitted fabric.

New yarn is labeled with information about how thick it is, known as its "symbol." The larger the number in the symbol, the thicker the yarn. Choose a yarn with the same symbol as the one used in your pattern. Selecting a heavier or lighter yarn symbol will result in a larger or smaller finished item.

Gauge

Another important consideration for the yarn you choose will be its suggested gauge. This is also specified on the label, with a symbol like the one shown here.

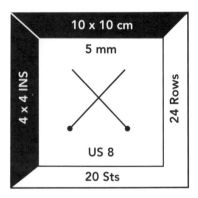

Gauge is always measured like this: Imagine a square of stockinette stitch knitting that is exactly 4" (10 cm) square. The gauge symbol is a simple drawing of that square. The needle drawing tells you what size needle the manufacturer suggests you use. The numbers specify how many stitches and how many rows will be in the square, when knitted with that size needle. In the example to the left, a 4" (10 cm) square of stockinette stitch knitting will contain 20 stitches per row and 24 rows, if you knit it with a size US 8 (5 mm) needle. It's important to choose yarn that fits the same gauge as that specified in your pattern, in order to get a finished project of the right size. Even after checking the gauge information, you'll still need to complete a gauge swatch of your own before beginning your project to make sure the needles you choose create the fabric you need.

Fiber

The next thing to think about is the fiber your yarn is made of. Different yarns are made from different fibers, or blends of fibers. Generally, fiber can be divided into three different categories: natural, manmade, and blends.

Natural fibers come either from the trimmed coats of animals or from plants. Wool, cashmere, silk, and alpaca are all examples of natural fibers derived from animals. Cotton, linen, and hemp all originate from plants.

Manmade fibers are derived from chemical mixtures made in textile factories. Examples of manmade fibers are acrylic, polyester, nylon, and rayon.

Blends are combinations of different fibers in varying amounts, trying to provide the best parts of each. Blended fibers can be made from any combination of natural and manmade fibers.

Besides the way each yarn feels, the most important consideration in choosing the fiber for your project will be how you care for it. Some fibers are machine washable and dryable, while others aren't. Some are delicate and require special care, while others are durable and hardwearing. Think about how your project will be cared for (and by whom!) as you consider the choices.

Measuring Tools

Fiberglass tape measure: For measuring bodies, not knitting. It's flexible to bend around heads, chests, etc.

Retractable tape measure: A miniature one from the hardware store, with a metal tape that has a hook on the end. For measuring knitting.

6" (13 cm) metal or plastic ruler: One with nice sharp edges and clear markings, for measuring gauge accurately.

Sewing Tools

Pins and needles: For marking gauge swatches and sewing on embellishments and closures.

Safety pins: For emergency stitch markers and holders.

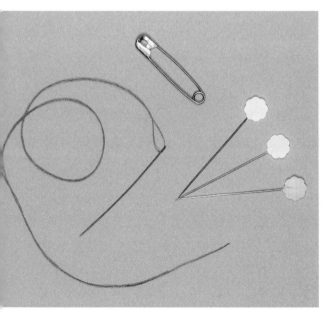

Knitting Tools

Stitch markers: Both opening and closed styles, for keeping track of rows and rounds.

Tapestry needles: Both bent- and straight-tip styles, with large eyes and blunt tips, for seaming knitted pieces and weaving in ends.

Crochet hook: For retrieving dropped stitches and fixing mistakes.

Needle size gauge: Handy for checking the sizes of unmarked needles.

Small, sharp sewing scissors: Better if they have a sheath to cover their blades.

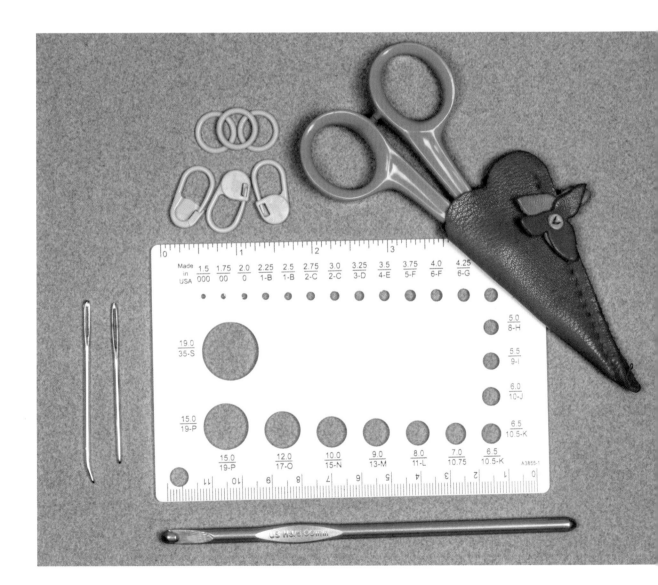

Techniques

How to Measure

Knitting instructions will most often tell you to knit until each piece reaches a certain length, rather than a particular number of rows. This is because even when you knit exactly to the same gauge, there can still be subtle differences in how many rows you get in the same length of knitting. To get accurate results, follow the same steps every time you measure, and for every piece.

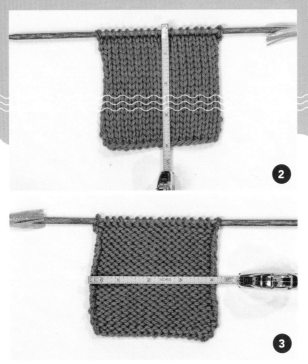

2

LAY THE KNITTING FLAT

1   Put it on a hard floor or table, rather than a carpet-ed or upholstered surface, and never measure your knitting in your lap. This is because any surface that yields to pressure (like a pillow) can give inconsistent measurements.

2   Using your retractable tape measure (see "Measuring Tools,' page 118), hook the end over the top of your needle, and measure down to the bottom edge of the piece.

3

3   Some stitch patterns are more challenging to mea-sure than others. Stockinette stitch, for example, is notoriously tricky because its edges curl in. To measure the width of a piece, try laying it wrong side up (with the purl side facing you). Place your tape measure from side to side in the middle of the piece to check its width.

How to Count Stitches and Rows

When working on gauge swatches, you'll be counting the number of stitches and rows in a 4" (10 cm) area. Counting them accurately is the only way to know whether you've obtained the gauge or not.

2

4

1   Lay the knitting flat as you did for taking measure-ments. (See previous steps above.)

2   Find the exact edge of a knitted stitch, and put a pin in it. With a 6" (15 cm) ruler (see "Measuring Tools," page 118), find the exact edge of a stitch in the same row, exactly 4" (10 cm) away, and put a second pin in it.

3   Leaving the ruler in place, carefully count all the stitches between pins. Pointing a knitting needle at each stitch and counting out loud can help with this step.

4   Now count the rows in 4" (10 cm) the same way (the stitches on your needle count as a row, too).

Cast On

In order to start knitting, you'll need to get a foundation row of stitches onto your needles. This is called casting on. There are many different ways to cast on, but we'll start with two: the cable cast on and the long-tail cast on. Almost every kind of cast on begins with a slipknot.

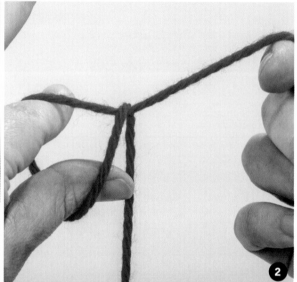

Slipknot

1 Make a loop in the end of your yarn, about 6" (13 cm) from the end.

2 Put your two fingers through the loop.

3 Grasp the strand (the one coming from the yarn ball, not the tail).

4 Pull the strand through the loop.

5 Pull the loop to tighten the knot around it.

6 Place the slipknot on your needle. Pull on the working strand to snug the slipknot up to the needle.

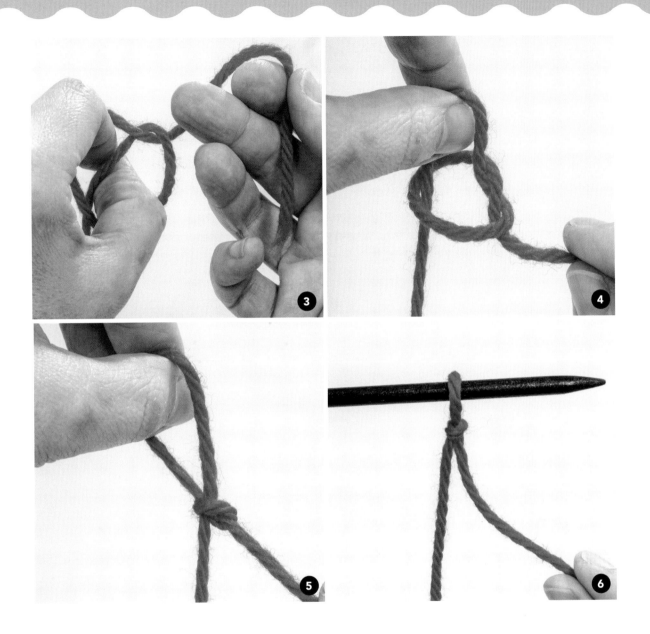

Cable Cast On

The cable cast on is named for the way its lower edge looks when complete—kind of like a twisted rope or cable. Here are the steps to do it:

1 Make a slipknot and place it on your needle.

2 Holding the needle with the slipknot in your left hand, place the point of the right needle through it, from front to back.

3 Wrap the yarn around and between the two needles, from back to front.

4 Use the point of the right needle to pull the strand through.

5 Without taking the slipknot off the left needle, pull the new stitch up and over onto the left needle.

6 For the next and all subsequent stitches, put the tip of the right needle between the last two stitches.

7 Repeat steps 3 through 6 until you have cast on all the stitches you need.

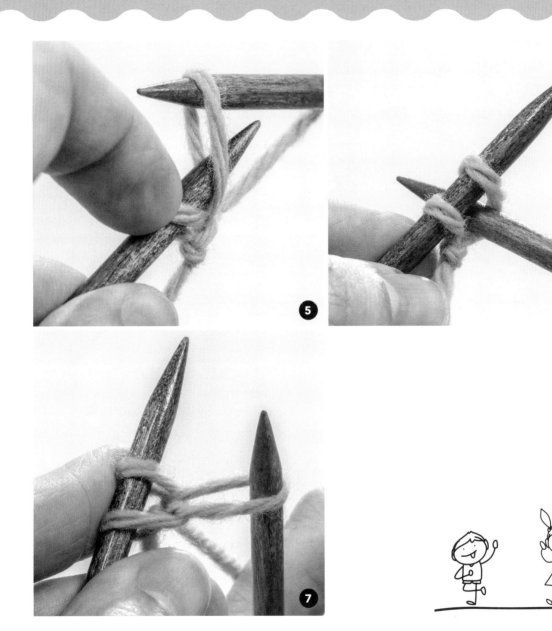

5

6

7

Knit

Once you have completed a row of cast-on stitches, you're ready to knit them. Here's how:

1 Hold the needle with the stitches to be worked in your left hand.

2 Put the right needle through the stitch, front to back.

3 Wrap the yarn around and between the needles, back to front.

4 Use the right needle to pull the strand through.

5 Let the old stitch come off the end of the left needle.

6 Repeat steps 2 through 5 until all the stitches from the left needle have been knitted onto the right needle. That's one row of knitting complete!

To knit another row, turn the needle with the stitches on it around so its point faces to the right. This is known as "turning the work." Now hold it with your left hand and switch the empty needle to your right hand. Knit the next row. Fabric made by knitting every stitch of every row is known as "garter stitch."

tip Especially when you are just starting out, try not to stop knitting until the entire row is complete. If you stop in the middle of the row, it can be hard to tell which direction you were going when you come back to knitting. If it can't be helped, try to remember which color needle was in each hand for when you come back.

Here's a rhyme to help you remember the steps for each knitted stitch:

In through the front door (step 2)
Around the back (step 3)
Out through the window (step 4)
And off jumps Jack (step 5)

Purl

Working a purl stitch is almost the same as working a knit stitch, with two important differences: 1. When purling, the working strand is held in front of the work, rather than in back, as in knitting. 2. When purling, the right needle goes into the stitch from back to front, rather than from front to back, as in knitting.

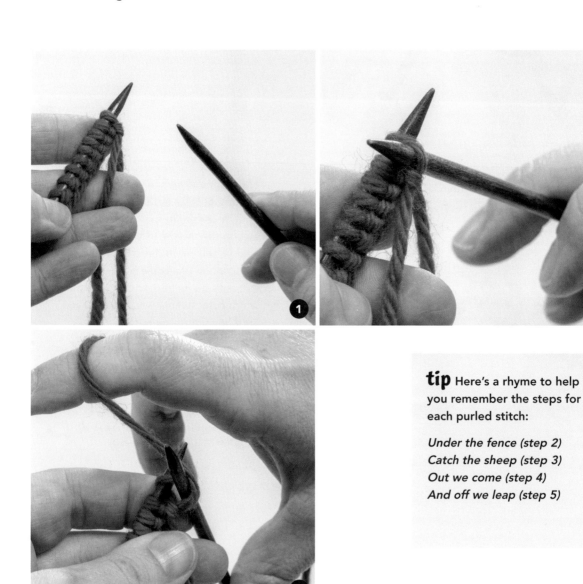

tip Here's a rhyme to help you remember the steps for each purled stitch:

Under the fence (step 2)
Catch the sheep (step 3)
Out we come (step 4)
And off we leap (step 5)

1 Hold the needle with the stitches to be worked in your left hand.

2 Put the right needle through the stitch, back to front.

3 Wrap the yarn around and between the needles, back to front.

4 Use the right needle to pull the strand through.

5 Let the old stitch come off the end of the left needle.

6 Repeat steps 2 through 5 until all the stitches from the left needle have been purled onto the right needle. That's one row of purling complete!

To purl another row, turn the needle with the stitches on it around so its point faces to the right. This is known as "turning the work." Now hold it in your left hand and switch the empty needle to your right hand. Purl the next row. Fabric made by purling every stitch of every row is known as "garter stitch."

If you knit one row, turn the work, and then purl the next row, you'll be working in "stockinette stitch," possibly the most common form of knitting. Try working alternating knit and purl rows a few times, to see how stockinette stitch (St st) is different from garter stitch.

Practice knitting complete rows, then purling complete rows, counting your stitches to make sure you have the same number you cast on. Keep practicing until you can work whole rows without any mistakes, dropped or added stitches. Once you're good at doing complete rows, practice switching between knit stitches and purl stitches, remembering to move the working yarn to the back between stitches for knitting, and to the front between stitches for purling.

Knit in the Round

Now that you understand the basics of flat knitting, it's time to try circular knitting, or knitting in the round. Worked with circular (circ) or double-pointed needles (DPN), knitting in the round creates cylindrical, tubular shapes, with no side edges. The diameter of the tube you knit is determined by the number of stitches you cast on. Short circular needles and double-pointed needles are used for smaller tubes (such as hats or sleeves), while longer circular needles are for larger tubes (like sweater bodies).

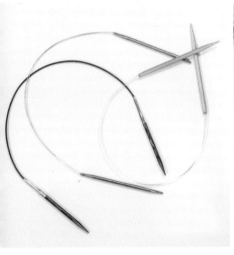

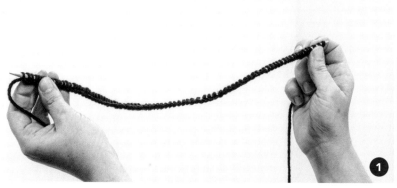

Join a Round

1 To begin knitting in the round, cast on as usual, using a circular needle. To start out, use a 16" (40.5 cm) -long circular needle in a size appropriate for your yarn. Once you have cast on all the stitches you need, add one more, extra stitch.

2 Lay your needle on a table with the tips pointed toward one another to make a circle. Keeping the needle as flat against the table as you can, twist the cast-on stitches so that the tops of the stitches (the loops) are all on the outside of the circle, and the bottoms of the stitches (the knots) are all on the inside of the circle.

3 Keeping the stitches arranged properly, carefully pick up the needles. Slip the first stitch on the right needle over to the left needle, where the tail is. Now knit the first two stitches on the left needle together (k2tog) to join the round.

Mark and Keep Track of Rounds

Once you knit an entire circle of stitches, you'll be back to the point where you joined the round. Place a marker (PM) between the last and the first stitch of the round.

From this point forward, if you knit every stitch, the fabric you get will be stockinette stitch, even though you never purled. This is the magic of circular knitting: there are no wrong side rows when you knit spiral tubes. Count the rows or measure the length of your piece only when you reach the marker, so you can be sure you've completely finished each round of knitting.

Bind Off

At the end of your knitting, you create a finished upper edge that won't unravel, by binding off. Knitted stitches should be bound off knitwise, and purled stitches should be bound off purlwise. This is known as binding off in pattern.

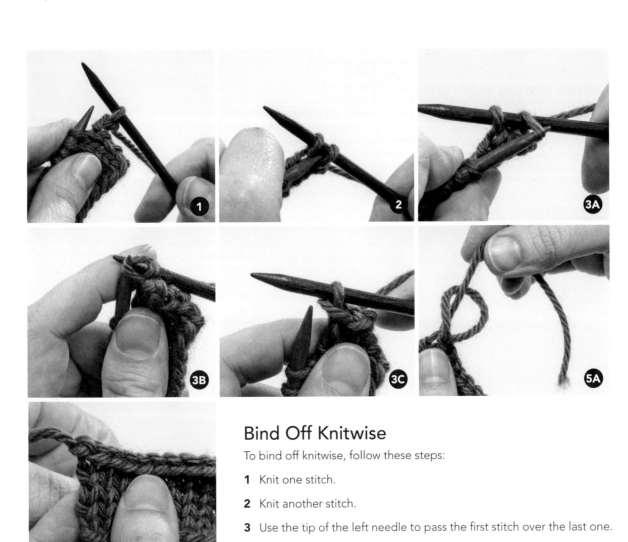

Bind Off Knitwise

To bind off knitwise, follow these steps:

1 Knit one stitch.

2 Knit another stitch.

3 Use the tip of the left needle to pass the first stitch over the last one.

4 Repeat steps 2 and 3 until all the stitches from the left needle are bound off, and only the last stitch remains on the right needle.

5 Break the yarn, leaving a tail of about 6" (13 cm). Pass the tail through the last stitch and pull gently to tighten.

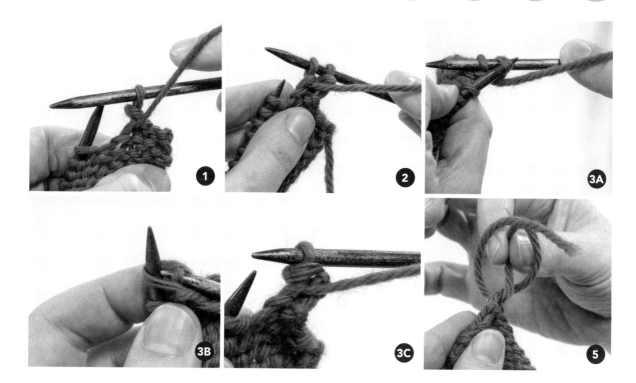

Bind Off Purlwise

To bind off purlwise, follow these steps:

1 Purl one stitch.

2 Purl another stitch.

3 Use the tip of the left needle to pass the first stitch over the last one.

4 Repeat steps 2 and 3 until all the stitches from the left needle are bound off, and only the last stitch remains on the right needle.

5 Break the yarn, leaving a tail of about 6" (13 cm). Pass the tail through the last stitch and pull gently to tighten.

Casting on, knitting, purling, and binding off are the most important skills in knitting. Take your time and have patience as you practice, remembering that mistakes are part of the process of learning. Here are a few more skills that will help you as you practice knitting and purling: frogging, tinking, and retrieving a dropped stitch.

Frogging

Knitters say that they "frog" their knitting when a big mistake happens and they "rip-it, rip-it." In other words, sometimes the best and fastest way to undo a mistake is to remove the needles from the knitting and pull on the working strand until the entire piece unravels. You can also frog just a few rows of knitting, say, back to just before the mistake, then put the needles carefully back into the live stitch loops. Don't be afraid to pull out mistakes; even the most experienced knitters do it all the time. Think of frogging as a great big eraser for your knitting mistakes. You'll only do it better the next time!

Tinking

Knit spelled backward is tink, and to tink means to "un-knit." When you notice a mistake made just a few stitches back, there's no need to remove the needles and rip out a lot of knitting. To tink, first turn the work so the newest stitches are on the left and the working yarn is coming from the left needle. Then, place the tip of your right needle into the stitch below the mistake, and pull gently on the working strand to unravel one stitch. Do this stitch by stitch, until you get back to the mistake, then fix it and continue on.

Retrieve a Dropped Stitch

When a stitch has accidentally fallen off the needle without being worked, it's said to have "dropped." You can tell this has happened when you count fewer stitches than you know you should have on your needle, and you can see where a "ladder" of stitches has formed in your fabric. Don't worry; you can pick up a dropped stitch again without having to frog your knitting. You'll need a crochet hook to do it most easily.

1 Locate the dropped stitch, and work up to where it should be on the needle.

2 Put the crochet hook into the loop of the dropped stitch, from front to back. Use the hook to pick up the next "ladder rung" above the stitch, then the next, and so on, until all the ladder rungs have been looped through one another. Check the back of your work to make sure you haven't skipped any rungs. Place the last rung on your left knitting needle, and continue knitting.

Decreases

K2tog (knit two together)

When pattern instructions call for you to "k2tog," you'll eliminate one stitch by creating a decrease that leans to the right.

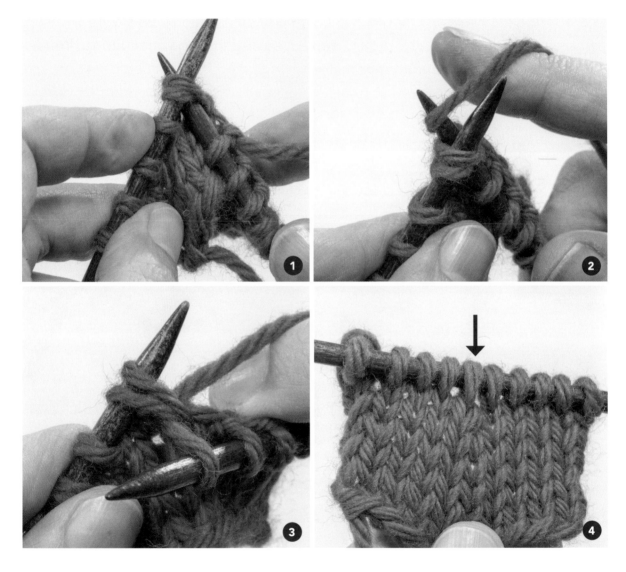

1 Work to the point where the pattern instructs you to k2tog, then put the tip of the right needle through the next two stitches at the same time.

2 Wrap the yarn as you normally would to knit.

3 Pull one new stitch through the two old ones.

4 Let the two stitches slip off the left needle. Continue knitting. You now have one stitch where there were two (arrow).

SSK (slip, slip, knit)

When pattern instructions call for you "SSK," you'll eliminate one stitch by creating a decrease that leans to the left.

1 Work to the point where the pattern instructs you to SSK, then slip one stitch to the right needle as if to knit it (knitwise).

2 Slip the next stitch to the right needle as if to knit it (knitwise).

3 Put the tip of the left needle into the fronts of the two stitches you just slipped.

4 Wrap the yarn and pull a new stitch through the two old ones, letting them slip off the left needle.

Increases

Kfb (knit into the front and back)

When pattern instructions call for you to "kfb," you'll make two stitches from one.

Knit into the stitch as you normally would, but don't slip it off the left needle yet.

Pivot your work toward you so that you can see the back leg of the stitch you just knitted into, then knit into it, too.

Let the original stitch slip off the left needle. You now have two stitches where there was one.

YO (yarn over)

When pattern instructions call for you to "yo," you'll make a new stitch by laying the working yarn over the top of the right needle between two stitches.

Knit to the point where the pattern instructs you to make a yarnover.

Bring the yarn to the front of the work between two stitches, then over the top of the right needle, and to the back again.

Continue knitting. The yo increase creates a hole in the knitting where the new stitch has formed.

Weave Ends

When you finish knitting, there will be yarn strands left over at the beginning and end of the piece, and sometimes in the middle, if you joined other colors or balls of yarn. To make the piece tidy, you just need to weave them in (we're using contrasting yarn here, so you can see it better).

1 To weave in cast-on and bind-off tails, thread the end of the yarn tail through a tapestry needle (see "Knitting Tools" on page 119).

2 Make stitches with the yarn tail through the edge of the knitting.

3 When the yarn tails are in the center of the piece, make stitches that follow the shape of the knitting.

4 Trim the yarn tail close to the knitting, being careful not to accidentally snip your knitted fabric. The weaving will be nearly invisible from the right side.

Blocking

To look its best, most knitted fabric needs some sort of finishing. Depending on the fiber it's made from, your yarn will need some combination of moisture, heat, and manipulation to lie flat and even up the stitches. Finishing your knitted fabric is referred to as blocking. Here are a few ways to block your knitting.

Steaming

Place your knitting flat on an ironing board and use the steam from an iron to gently moisten and warm it. Leave it on the ironing board to dry, with pins to hold it in shape, if needed. When steaming your knitting, be careful not to touch the iron to the knitted fabric; hold it 2" to 3" (5 to 7.6 cm) away at all times. And of course, never touch the sole plate of the iron, or put your hand in the way of the steam.

tip Safety first! If you are under ten, have an adult handle the iron for you. If you are over ten, get an adult to supervise you when handling an iron.

Washing

Fill a basin with warm (not hot) water and add a small amount of detergent suitable for washing wool. Add your knitting to the bath, gently pressing to remove all the air bubbles. Let it soak for at least 20 minutes. Gently squeeze the water out, without twisting or wringing. Lay the piece flat to dry, reshaping to the blocking measurements in your pattern's schematic, if necessary. (A schematic is a line drawing of the pieces drawn to scale, with accompanying measurements. Each drawing corresponds to each section to be knitted.) If your finished piece has straight edges, be sure to straighten them by pinning them down to a carpeted floor, an ironing board, or a blocking mat while it's still damp. (A blocking mat is a piece of waterproof material, usually rubber or foam, on which knitting is laid to dry.) Make sure your knitting has dried completely before proceeding.

Misting

Lay your knitting on a moisture-safe surface, such as a towel or blocking mat. Mist it with a spray bottle until the surface is damp, but not soaking wet. Straighten and shape the piece, using pins and consulting your pattern's schematics for measurements, if needed.

To choose the best blocking technique for your project, pay close attention to the care instructions provided on your yarn label. However they instruct you to care for the finished garment, that's a safe way for how to block your piece. For example, if your yarn's care instructions say "Hand wash in warm water, lay flat to dry," then that's probably a good method to block your knitting, too.

Favorite Washcloth

Hand knitted washcloths are wonderful to use, because they get softer and softer with age. They are also quick and fun to knit, which makes them excellent for gift giving. Washcloths are so popular to make that many yarn companies keep a line of cotton washcloth yarns in their collections at all times. This project will help you practice yo (yarn over) increases, k2tog (knit two together) decreases, and garter stitch knitting. Be warned, though—once you start making washcloths, you (and the people you give them to) might get hooked on them!

You will need

Yarn

 Medium

SHOWN: Kitchen Cotton by Lion Brand, 100% cotton, 2 oz (57 g)/99 yd (91 m): Kiwi #831-170, 1 skein

Needles

- Size 8 (5 mm) straight or size to obtain gauge

Notions

- Tapestry needle

Gauge

18 sts and 36 rows = 4" (10 cm) in garter st

Take time to check gauge.

Sizes

Finished measurements: 9½" (24 cm) tall, 9½" (24 cm) wide

Construction

Washcloth is worked diagonally from point to point, back and forth in rows.

Stitch Guide

GARTER STITCH: Knit every st, every row.

Washcloth

CO 4 sts. Knit 2 rows.

Increases

Inc row: *K2, yo, knit to end of row—1 st inc'd.
Rep inc row every row 55 more times—60 sts.

Decreases

Dec row: *K1, k2tog, yo, k2tog, knit to end of row—
1 st dec'd.
Rep dec row every row 53 more times—6 sts.

Next row: K1, [k2tog] 2 times, k1—4 sts.
Knit 2 rows. BO.

Finishing

Weave in ends. Block to measurements.

tip To make a yarn over (yo), bring the working yarn forward between the needles, then lay it from front to back over the top of the right needle. That's all there is to it!

Cowl

Cowls are terrific for practicing knitting in the round. They take much less time to make than scarves, but provide the same cuddly function! Try this one to master k2, p2 rib, and stockinette in the round.

You will need

Yarn

 Medium

SHOWN: Longwood by Cascade Yarns, 100% superwash ex-trafine merino wool, 3.5 oz (100 g)/191 yd (175 m): Plum #28 (MC) and Green Olive #15 (CC), 1 skein each

Needles

- Size 7 (4.5 mm) 16" (40 cm) circular
- Size 8 (5 mm) 16" (40 cm) circular or size to obtain gauge

Notions

- Stitch marker
- Tapestry needle

Gauge

20 sts and 27 rnds = 4" (10 cm) in St st on larger needle

Take time to check gauge.

Sizes

Finished measurements: 18½" (47 cm) circumference, 10" (25.5 cm) high

Construction

Cowl is worked circularly, in rounds, from bottom to top.

Stitch Guide

K2, P2 RIB: *K2, p2; rep from * to end of rnd.

STOCKINETTE STITCH (ST ST): Knit every st, every rnd.

Cowl

With smaller needle, CC, and using the cable CO method, CO 92 sts. Pm and join for working in rnds, being careful not to twist. Work in k2, p2 rib until piece measures 1" (2.5 cm) from CO. Break yarn and join MC. With larger needle, work in St st until piece measures 9" (23 cm) from CO. Break yarn and join CC. Knit 1 rnd. Work in k2, p2 rib until piece measures 10" (25.5 cm) from CO. BO loosely in patt.

Finishing

Weave in ends. Steam lightly to block.

Cast On, page 122
Knit in the Round, page 130
Knit, page 126
Purl, page 128
Bind Off, page 132
Weave Ends, page 139
Blocking, page 140

tip "Binding off in pattern" means that you work each stitch in the bind off as it was worked in the prior round: bind off knit stitches knitwise, and bind off purl stitches purlwise.

Pencil Roll

This project will help you understand more about gauge. Most of the time in knitting, we match the weight of our yarns to the size of our needles in order to knit fabric that is neither too stiff nor too floppy. But what if we need a tighter or a looser fabric? In this project, the finished fabric needs to be firmer and denser, to keep the pencil points from poking through. To achieve that, we can intentionally choose to knit medium-weight yarn on fine needles. The resulting fabric is thicker and firmer than it would be with bigger needles. The finished piece holds twelve pencils (or pens), plus erasers or other items in the widest slot.

Gauge

26 sts and 36 rows = 4" (10 cm) in St st

Take time to check gauge.

Sizes

Finished measurements: 15" (38 cm) wide, 13" (33 cm) high (7" [18 cm] high when folded)

Construction

Pencil roll is worked in one piece, back and forth in rows.

Stitch Guide

STOCKINETTE STITCH (ST ST): RS rows: Knit. WS rows: Purl.

SEED STITCH: RS rows: *K1, p1; rep from * to end of row. WS rows: *P1, k1; rep from * to end of row.

You will need

Yarn

4 Medium

SHOWN: Classic Wool Worsted by Patons, 100% wool, 3.5 oz (100 g)/210 yd (192 m): Royal Blue #77132 (MC), 1 skein; Peacock #00218 (CC), 1 skein

Needles

• Size 3 (3.25 mm) straight or size to obtain gauge

Notions

• Tapestry needle

• Hand sewing needle and thread

• Pins

• 1 yd (1 m) of ⅝" (16 mm) ribbon (shown: May Arts EH16 Olive/ Lime)

• **OPTIONAL:** One size 3/0 (¼" [6 mm]) snap

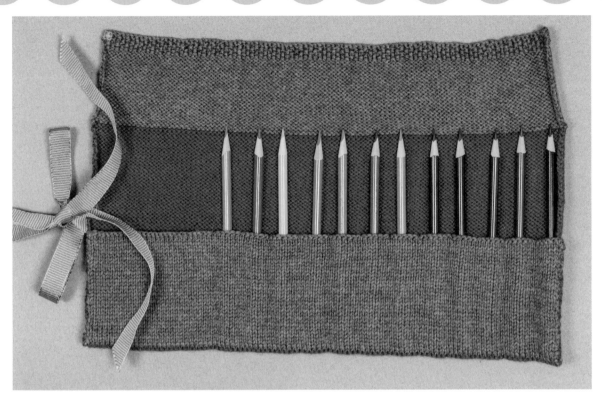

Pencil Roll

Lower Flap

With CC, CO 100 sts. Work in St st until piece measures 3½" (9 cm) from CO, ending with a WS row.

Back

Break yarn and join MC. Purl 1 RS row, forming turning ridge on RS. Work in St st until piece measures 7" (18 cm) from color change, ending with a WS row.

Upper Flap

Break yarn and join CC. Purl 1 RS row, forming turning ridge on RS. Work in St st until flap measures 2¼" (6 cm) from color change, ending with a WS row. Work 4 rows in seed st. BO in patt.

Finishing

Weave in ends and block. Fold lower flap up and pin in place, matching sides. Sew edges tog at both ends (see illustration). Beg at far right, measure 1" (2.5 cm) from edge and mark with a pin. Cont placing pins as shown to mark 12 small slots and one large one. Sew through both layers as shown with matching thread, knotting securely at both ends.

Fold the top flap down and roll from right to left. Fold ribbon about 15" (38 cm) from end and pin in place at left edge of roll. Sew ribbon in place securely.

tip If the left corner of the upper flap sticks out when the roll is closed, add a small snap to secure it (see illustration below).

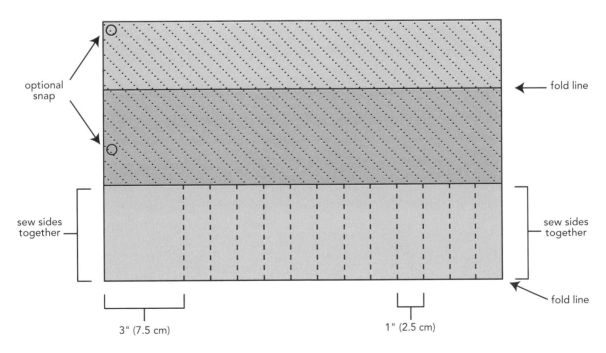

optional snap

fold line

sew sides together

sew sides together

fold line

3" (7.5 cm)

1" (2.5 cm)

Sewing

Have you ever been having sew much fun you didn't realize you were building your skills? Join us as we take you from the basics of hand stitching to the fun of machine sewing and off to the world of creative design! As you are learning new skills you will be making projects that are exciting and fun. Once you learn the basics, you can add your own design elements and embellishments, which increase not only your knowledge and skills, but the fun factor as well! When you become comfortable sewing simple projects, you will then move on to creating items just for you!

This section offers a unique view of sewing, which needs your creativity and imagination to see how far you can go. A simple task of stitching a chenille pot holder can expand into making a chenille rug for your pet—or even one for your room! After completing a technique and project, think of how to expand, change, or embellish it. Your imagination will become the focus as you move through the book and build your skills and confidence.

Your job is to believe in yourself. You'll learn about the tools you will need, the machine you will use, and how to organize your sewing tools. In addition, you'll learn how to be safe while using the machine and sewing tools. All the techniques and know-how can be learned in this book while having fun.

The more you know, the more fun it is to sew.

The more you sew, the more you will know!

As you begin to sew, you will be using tools that, perhaps, you have never seen or used before. Although we will describe the correct way to use these tools and give you tips on safety, it will be up to you and your parents to discuss what they feel comfortable with you using—whether it will be alone, with adult supervision, or with adult assistance. It is important to keep in mind that many of these tools are pointy, sharp, or hot, and you will need to remain focused as you use them. Always ask for help if you are unsure.

Like the rest of the book, this chapter features several projects, all of which have suggestions and tips on how to make it your own through embellishment and design. Throughout this section are tips that will explain special methods and offer ideas or refer you to a page where you can learn more. We hope you find this system easy to use so all the information you need is at your fingertips.

—*Janith Bergeron and Christine Ecker*

Materials and Tools

Fabric and Fibers

Types

The following offers a brief description of fabrics and fibers used in this book. It by no means is a complete list of what you may find or choose to use. Pretesting is always recommended. Fabrics can be woven, knit, or felted.

Batik Light- and medium-weight cotton or rayon. Resist dyeing creates beautiful designs.

Canvas A heavy-duty woven. It can be used as a stabilizer.

Cotton A versatile woven fabric whose fibers come from the cotton plant.

Corduroy A woven fabric with ridges that run the length of the fabric. These ridges can range from very fine to a wide-wale corduroy. It is strong and wears well. The nap is important. If cutting multiple pieces, make sure the nap goes in the same direction.

Denim A strong cotton fabric. Pretreating is important.

Felt This is a nonwoven made of pressed fibers. Wool felt is pressed with 100% wool fibers or wool and synthetic fibers. Craft felt can be thick and strong or weak and flimsy and is pressed synthetic fibers.

Fleece This synthetic material is lightweight and provides warmth. It doesn't fray or shrink.

Fusible Interfacing This material is either woven or pressed fibers with the addition of adhesive (glue). It is used to stabilize a thin material or add body and stiffness to areas of garments (such as collars and cuffs). Fusible interfacing is pressed onto the wrong side of the fabric using a hot iron and a press cloth. Enough heat and pressure are required to melt the adhesive or puckers will appear and the interfacing will not be effective.

Fusible Web This material comes in sheets or in a roll of various widths and has a paper back to protect the glue surface. It has many uses and is very helpful in appliqué work. It is fused onto the wrong side of the design, the paper is removed, and the design is then fused to the project.

Knit This nonwoven material ranges from thin T-shirt to thick sweatshirt fabric, and is stretchy.

Muslin A plain-weave fabric, muslin is usually made from cotton or a cotton blend. It is sold in a variety of qualities.

Nonwoven Fabric These materials are made of pressed fibers and have no grain lines. Examples include fleece and felt.

Polyester This fabric is made from synthetic fibers (petroleum-based products). Most are not biodegradable. Beware that you must use a cool/warm iron and a low dryer temperature, or polyester can melt.

Sew-in Interfacing This is an interfacing that must be sewn into the garment when making seams, unlike the fusible interfacing, which is fused with adhesive to the garment using a hot iron.

Woven Fabric This material contains warp fibers (threads put onto a loom before the fabric is woven) and weft fibers (threads woven across and through the warp fibers).

Working with Fabric

Raw Edge The raw edge of fabric is the cut edge, and this is prone to fraying or unraveling. Take care to finish off the raw edges.

Selvage (or Selvedge) The selvage is the edge of the fabric. Some selvage edges are printed with information about the manufacturer or company or even offer little dots displaying the colors used in the fabric. The selvages are often more tightly woven and can shrink at a different rate from the fabric, so they should be cut off and not used as part of a project.

Directional Designs If you are working with a print, take a careful look at the direction of the design. Designs can go one way (such as letters), two ways (such as stripes), or in any direction (such as polka dots). The distance from one design to the next is called a repeat.

Nap This is a texture on the surface of the fabric. It is smooth in one direction and rough in the opposite direction. Make sure the nap goes in the same direction when piecing fabric together.

Grain Line The grain line describes the direction in which the fibers line up in the fabric. It's important to cut out pieces from material in the way the pattern directs, because it will affect how much the fabric stretches. Straight of grain means the cuts are made parallel to the selvage edge, and this will give the strongest piece of material with little, if any, stretch. Cross grain means the cuts are made from selvage edge to selvage edge (the opposite of straight of grain) and has a bit of stretch. Bias means cutting on the diagonal of the fabric (corner to corner), and it has the most stretch.

Pretreating It's important to wash and dry a fabric before you use it because most fabrics shrink. Less expensive fabrics have a "sizing," or stiffening agent, such as starch, added to them. Sizing washes out, often leaving fabrics thin and limp and not acceptable for certain projects. Some fabrics may need to be dry-cleaned, depending on the fiber.

Zippers If your project calls for a zipper, it will specify which type of zipper to use. All-purpose zippers (right) do not separate at the bottom, and they come in different weights to suit the project. Separating zippers (left) come apart in two pieces. Zippers like the white one shown have teeth that are intended to be exposed.

You can shorten an all-purpose zipper by creating a new zipper stop at the desired length. Center the closed zipper under the presser foot, set the machine stitch length to 0 and the stitch width to the widest setting. Using your handwheel, zigzag five times over the zipper teeth to create a bar tack. Trim the excess zipper tape using an old scissors.

PARTS OF A ZIPPER

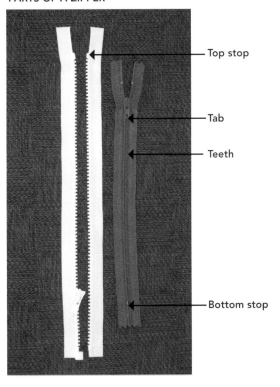

Top stop

Tab

Teeth

Bottom stop

Tool Kit

Many of the tools and materials you'll need are listed on these and the following pages. You might not use all the materials and tools pictured in the projects that follow, but they are handy to know about for future projects.

Needles and Pins

Machine Needles (A) Needles are important to understand and as you sew you will learn more and more about why they are shaped a certain way and which needles sew best on which fabrics with which threads. For now, it is important to remember that needles are disposable. They will get dull, bend, and even break at times! You should change your needle after every eight hours of sewing, more often if you are having trouble with missed stitches or frayed and broken thread, or are sewing on specialty fabrics.

When you are sewing on woven fabrics you will use a "sharp" class of needle and when you sew on knits or things that stretch you will use a "ball" or "stretch" needle. Needles range in size, with the smaller number needles used for lighter weight fabrics while sewing with finer threads. Heavyweight fabrics use a larger needle, which can accommodate a heavier weight thread. There are also twin needles, triple needles, and double-eye needles, as well as needles for metallics, embroidery thread, and leather, plus many, many more! You should use the correct needle for the project at hand.

Pins: (B) Pins come in a variety of sizes with different shaped heads. Sturdy pins approximately 1¾" (4.5 cm) long with round heads are helpful when you are beginning to sew. This will give you something substantial to grasp as you learn how to pin, and they will not bend as easily as some other pins. However, they have plastic heads that will melt, so be careful when pressing. Other types of pins include glass head pins,

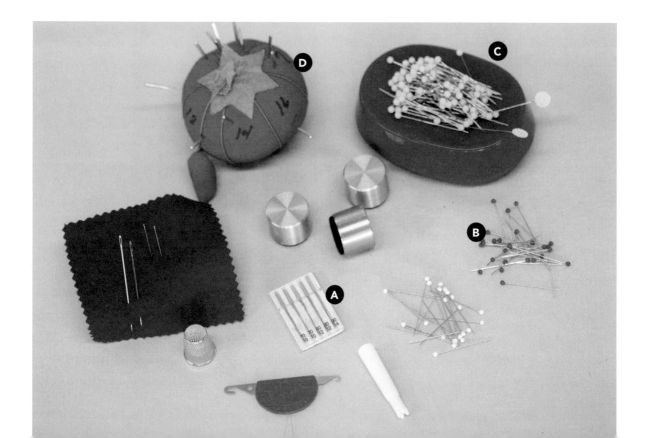

which will not melt when used at the iron, and flower head pins, which have larger heads that are flat and easy to see, making it easier to put a ruler over them when measuring. The flower head pins also hold lace and loosely woven fabrics without having the head slip through the holes. Whatever type of pin you use, the important thing to remember is to discard your bent and dull pins.

Magnetic Pin Cushion (C) This is a great way to store your pins. It's easy to use and great for picking up if you drop any!

Tomato Needle/Pin Holder (D) Mark needle sizes on the sections of a tomato-shaped cushion and you will always know where to find the correct needle!

Thread

Thread The type and weight of thread is chosen based on the fabric that you are using. Thread is made of fibers that are twisted together. Higher quality thread is made of fibers that are long, making the thread strong and smooth. Poorer quality thread is made of shorter fibers, which weaken it, allowing it to break and fray more easily. It can also cause the thread to have a fuzzy look, so if you use it to topstitch a seam it can look unfocused. Make sure you use a quality thread instead of bargain thread to have more success and less frustration.

Cutting Tools

Scissors You will need two pairs of good-quality scissors in your sewing basket: one pair of angled shears approximately 8" (20 cm) long and a short pair of scissors about 5" (12.5 cm) long. The shears are used to cut your fabric and the shorter scissors are for thread cutting and smaller cuts on fabric like trimming corners. Both of these scissors should only be used on fabric! Cutting paper with them will dull them and make it hard to cut your fabric precisely. It is a good idea to have a pair of paper scissors in your tool kit as well. Snips are very small scissors that are used just for clipping threads. Zipper scissors are the pair of old scissors you use to trim across the zipper teeth. This will ruin the scissors, so it is usually the oldest pair of scissors you can find!

Rotary Cutter (A) A rotary cutter, gridded mat, and gridded ruler are used together to cut fabric with nice clean edges. This is a time-saving way to cut, but it does take a bit of practice. When you purchase a rotary cutter, it is best if you buy one that automatically retracts the blade when you release the grip. Use the grids on the mat to line up your fabric along a straight edge, lay your ruler on top of the fabric, and make sure you check that the ruler is lined up on your guidelines at the top *and* the bottom. It is easy to cut a crooked line if you don't check both. To hold the ruler in place, use the pads of your finger and thumb to create five points of pressure. This will hold your

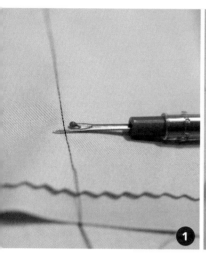
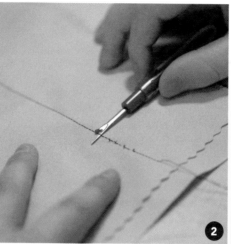
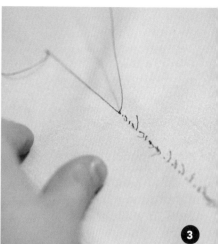

ruler in place better and be safer than placing the palm of your hand on the ruler. Press the grip of your rotary cutter and squeeze to engage the blade. Place one finger on top of the rotary cutter to gain the proper pressure as you cut. Starting just off the beginning of your fabric, place the blade flush against the ruler. Press firmly and start rolling along the ruler to cut your fabric. Use a smooth forward motion and resist sawing back and forth. You should always cut away from or across your body, never toward it. Rotary cutters are very sharp and should only be used with adult supervision.

Pinking Shears (B) Pinking shears are scissors that have a blade made up of points so that when it cuts your fabric it makes a zigzag edge. This is an easy way to finish the raw edge of your fabric to reduce fraying. Another option for pinking edges is a wave rotary cutter blade.

Seam Rippers (C) Seam rippers are used to unstitch seams that didn't sew correctly or are in the wrong spot. Seam rippers have a blade in the curved area near the pointed end and usually have a ball to protect your fabric from getting snagged. They are disposable and should be discarded when the blade becomes dull and you have to start pushing too hard to cut the thread. The best way to rip a seam—putting the least amount of stress on your fabric and leaving the smallest holes—is to lay it flat, slip the point of the seam ripper under a stitch (1), and gently push away from you to cut the threads (don't pull up on your seam ripper or you can poke your eye!). Cut every three or four stitches (and every backtack stitch) (2). Turn the fabric over and pull the thread, "unzipping" the seam (3).

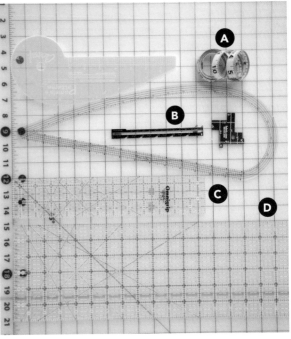

Pressing Tools

Iron and Ironing Board You will need a good iron and an ironing board to make your projects look as professional as possible. An iron is very hot and should only be used with adult supervision. Never leave the iron lying flat on the ironing board, as it will burn if left too long. It is important to take care not to scratch the soleplate (bottom) of your iron. An iron that steams from the bottom is preferable to one that sprays water out the front.

Pressing correctly and taking the time to do it well will do as much for your project's appearance as stitching a straight seam. Remember that before you cut your fabric, it is okay to *iron* your material, meaning you can move your iron around and slide it on top of the fabric. Once you have cut the fabric out, you will need to *press* your fabric by lifting the iron off the fabric when you move it to a different place so as not to distort or stretch the fabric.

Press Cloth Silk organza or a polyester-organza blend are great because you can see through them and they can withstand high heat. An old, clean cotton handker-chief will do in a pinch. Using a press cloth protects your fabrics. When fusing interfacing it will keep your iron clean, and it can be laundered.

Measuring Tools

Measuring Tape (A) A flexible 60" (152 cm) fiberglass tape measure is used to measure around the body.

Hem Gauge (B) A hem gauge is a handy tool for easy marking and can be used at the iron as well. It is easy to move the blue slider to hold your measurement.

Gridded Ruler (C) Gridded rulers come in many sizes and usually have 1" (2.5 cm) squares to help line things up. They are easy to read and are sometimes used with rotary cutters and gridded mats. (See Rotary Cutter on page 160). Beware that "quilter's rulers" sometimes add ¼" (6 mm) seam allowances to the rulers.

Gridded Mat (D) A large gridded mat will help you measure accurately and "square" things up. It is a great workspace for cutting and pinning.

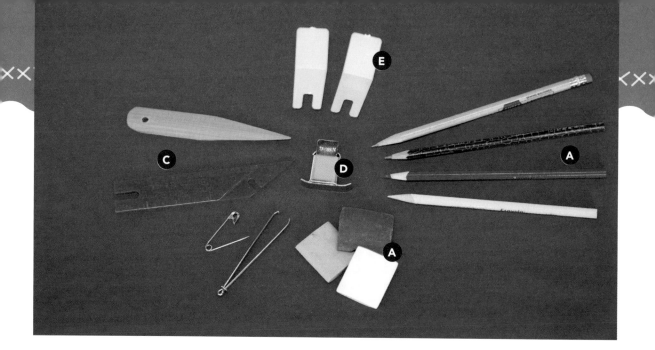

Other Handy Tools

Marking Tools (A) There are a variety of marking tools out there; some work great and others not so much. We have found that when you are marking your fabric, generally a regular pencil or colored pencil will work and comes out easily. If you are marking somewhere on your project that may show (e.g., darts, placement lines, etc.), you should use tailor's chalk, which does not have any wax in it and will brush off fabric easily. Most important is to test your marking tool on a scrap of your fabric to make sure it will come out easily.

Point Turner (C) Point turners are used to reach into corners and points to make them the proper shape. You can use the rounded side to ease curves into their natural shape as well as running along straight seams to straighten them out, thus making pressing easier. Point turners come in bamboo or plastic.

Magnetic Seam Guide (D) A magnetic seam guide can be a help if you are having difficulty staying on a certain seam allowance marking on your machine. You can place the magnetic guide at the seam allowance mark on your throat plate and butt the fabric up against it to stay on the line. Do not use magnets on computerized machines.

Hump Jumper (E) A Hump Jumper can help you go more easily over thick seams or uneven fabrics. It slips under your presser foot to raise it to the level of thick fabric and allow your machine to stitch better.

Tool Box A medium-size, clear plastic food container works well for a tool kit.

Standard Sewing Tool Box

Scissors
Pins
Needles
Hem gauge
Measuring tape
Thread
Marking tools
Seam ripper

Getting to Know Your Machine

First, identify key parts of your machine and understand how they work. Sit at your machine with your owner's manual and refer to the Appendix in the back of this book entitled "Sewing Machine" to explore the parts of your machine and see how they move. It is best if you do this with a machine that is not threaded so that you will not run into tangles and can focus more clearly on the machine itself. Obviously, when you get to threading the machine and seeing how a stitch is formed you will need to thread your machine. If you do not have a manual, most can be downloaded from the Internet. Remember that proper maintenance and frequent cleaning of your machine will keep it running smoothly, which will translate into more fun for you!

Once you have explored your machine parts, practiced using your foot pedal, wound a bobbin, and threaded your machine, it is time to talk about putting it all together!

If you come across something you are not familiar with or wish to know more about, chances are it will be in the Appendix: information on the sewing machine, a tool kit, and understanding fabrics and fibers are at your fingertips. Taking a quick walk through these pages will allow you to get up and running with the fewest problems.

We'll practice some stitching on paper and learn some basic techniques. Then you can move on to the first project.

Tips for Success

- When you start to sew a seam, make sure your thread tails are under the presser foot and that your presser foot is down.

- *Always* make sure the take-up lever is in the highest position when you begin and end a seam! Three clues the take-up lever is not at its highest point:

    A The fabric is hard to pull out of the machine.

    B More than two threads are attached to the fabric.

    C The needle keeps coming unthreaded.

- Press your foot pedal slowly to start so that your thread is not jerked quickly, which may cause it to get looped around something.

- If you have to reverse, stop your machine completely and press your reverse button firmly to change directions. You will usually need to hold your reverse button down the whole time you wish to sew backward.

- Remember your feed dogs! They are there to move the fabric through your machine. Your job is to steer and keep things where you want them.

- If your machine is making strange noises, stop and make sure it is threaded and sewing properly.

- If you are having a hard time staying on your seam line, you can use a magnetic seam guide or a piece of low-tack tape (such as painter's tape) to help you. *Do not use a magnetic guide on a computerized machine!*

- If you turn your fabric over and see many loops along your seam line, generally that means your bobbin is not in correctly. Sometimes it means the machine is not correctly threaded through all the tension guides and take-up lever.

- Remember that stitching takes practice and embrace it, even if it involves unstitching. Your seam ripper is your friend!

Safety Tip

When you change broken or dull needles or discard bent pins or dull rotary blades, *don't* throw them in the trash! Put them in a lidded container—a small box or jar—that you can keep in your sewing room. When the container is full, cover it and throw it away.

Techniques

Paper Stitching Practice

These first exercises will help you become more comfortable and proficient at the sewing machine. You will be working on paper without the machine threaded, learning some of the language of sewing, and practicing controlling your machine. Practicing without thread at first allows you to focus on the process without worrying about any thread tangles or other issues.

Dry Run

Directions

Notes: For safety reasons, when you are not sewing, keep your foot off the pedal. Sometimes, when you are adjusting your fabric and lining things up, you can accidentally lean on the foot pedal, making the machine run, and you don't want your fingers to be near the needle if this happens.

You will need

Tools

- size 80/12 needle

Other Supplies

- paper for practice

Patterns

- straight stitch
- pivot
- slow curve

1   First, let's look at posture and machine positioning. Proper posture at the machine is important not only for your body but also for the quality of your stitching. Sit centered in front of the needle so that you can clearly see your seam allowances and more easily direct your fabric. Sit up straight and try not to lean on the table with your forearms or elbows because this limits the motion of your hands and can make your stitching "jerky." Place your foot pedal a comfortable distance away from you where you can reach it and press without lifting your heel off the floor. Try sewing barefoot or in soft-soled shoes so that you can more easily feel the pedal, and thus have more control over your sewing.

2   With your hands in your lap, practice pressing the pedal to go slower and faster. Keep your heel on the floor to anchor your foot and control your speed better. When you want to take just a stitch or two, rest your foot on the pedal and just curl your big toe. Sit on the edge of your chair if it helps you reach the pedal. If you still have a hard time reaching the pedal correctly, then it is okay to put the pedal on a box. When you feel you have control over the pedal, you are ready to move on to practice on paper.

Techniques you'll need

- How to thread the machine and insert the bobbin
- How to run your machine

You will learn

- How to properly feed paper or fabric through the machine
- How to maintain steady hand pressure
- How to sew a straight line
- How to backtack
- How to sew a curved line

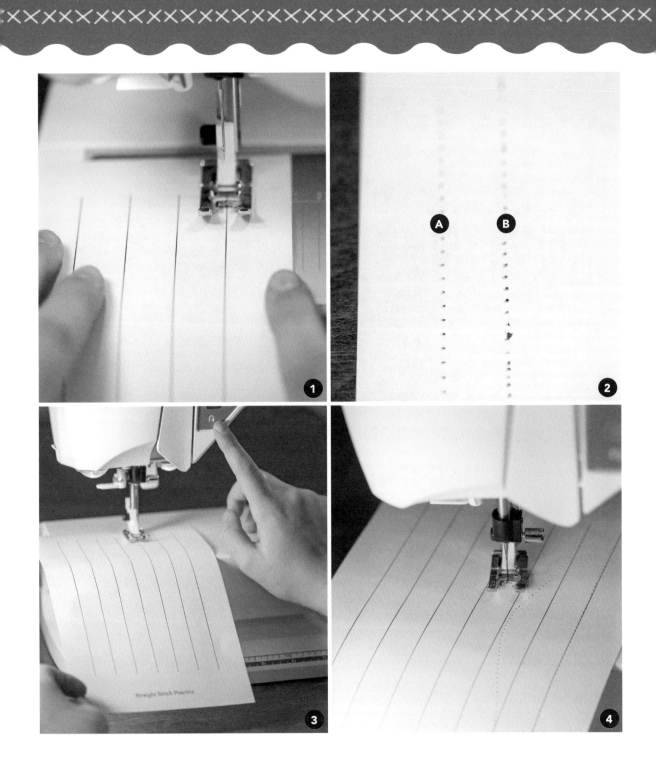

Straight Stitching

Directions

1 Copy the straight stitch template on page 186. Lift your presser foot and line up your paper so that the first line is centered at your needle. Lower your presser foot. You will complete this first line without using your hands! Your machine may or may not stay on the line, but that will not matter. With hands in your lap, gently press your foot pedal and sew to the end of the line. Take your foot off the pedal and turn the handwheel toward you until the thread take-up lever and needle are in their highest position. Lift your presser foot and remove the paper. Turn your paper over to see what kinds of holes were made. Your paper should have round, evenly spaced holes where your needle has sewn. This will be your goal when you begin to put your hands on the paper to steer.

2 Line up your paper on the next line. This time put your hands lightly on the paper to steer it. Keep your hands in front of the needle to steer from the front instead of pulling from the back. Keep your eye just in front of the presser foot to make sure you have time to make adjustments if needed. Gently press your foot pedal and stitch from the top of the line to the bottom, trying to stay on the line. No fair lifting your presser foot and moving your paper over if you get off the line! Try to gently steer back on if you drift off. Remove the paper and turn it over to look at the holes. If your hand pressure was good, your holes should be round and even (A). If you have too much hand pressure or are pulling your paper instead of gently steering, your holes will be distorted, uneven, and much closer together (B).

3 On the next line you will learn how to backtack. Backtacking prevents the beginning and ending stitches from coming loose. To backtack, start down just a bit from the beginning point and reverse two or three stitches, then stitch forward to sew your seam. When you get to the end, backtack by reversing two or three stitches to secure.

4 Line up your needle on the next line and you will learn how to steer with a practice curve. Stitch a short distance, then start to curve off to the right until you touch the line next to it, and then steer back onto your original line. After you have practiced this direction, do a line or two curving off to the left. These are important to practice until you are comfortable with steering to where you want to go. Remember to check your holes on the back of the paper to learn more about your hand pressure and whether you are tugging the paper into position (uneven, distorted holes) or steering it (even, round holes).

Tip ALWAYS check to make sure your take-up lever and needle are in their highest position before lifting the presser foot and removing paper or fabric. If they are not in the highest position, turn the handwheel toward you until they are.

Seam Allowances

These exercises will get you familiar with seam allowances. A seam allowance is the distance from the edge of your fabric to the seam. Seam allowance widths are marked on the throat plate of your machine (see page 163 for details). The most common seam allowances and their general uses are ¼" (6 mm) for quilting, ⅜" (1 cm) for craft sewing, ½" (1.3 cm) for home décor sewing, and ⅝" (1.6 cm) for garments. Please remember this is just a general outline. Your pattern will tell you the actual seam allowance required. For the seam allowance exercise, you will need a blank 5" x 7" (12.5 x 17.8 cm) piece of paper.

Notes: For this exercise, we will be using the edge of the general purpose presser foot as the guide for ¼" (6 mm) seam allowance. On some sewing machines, this is pretty accurate; on others it may be a bit wider than ¼" (6 mm). When you really need an exact ¼" (6 mm) seam allowance, such as for quilting, you may need to purchase a special presser foot.

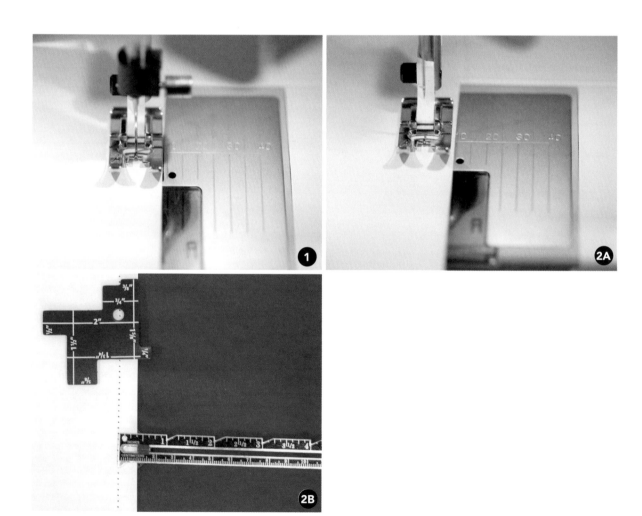

Directions

Notes: Sewing on paper is great practice, but it will dull the machine needle, so be sure to change to a new needle before moving on to a fabric project. For sewing on paper, use an older needle that is dull but not bent!

1 For this exercise, we will be using the edge of your presser foot as ¼" (6 mm). Line up one edge of the paper with the right edge of your presser foot, just down from the top edge of the paper. Begin the seam by reversing two or three stitches for your backtack, and then continue down the edge of the paper, using the edge of your presser foot as your guide. Your eye should be looking at the edge of the presser foot, not the needle. Backtack at the end of the paper.

2 Choose a different edge of the paper and line it up using the ⅜" (1 cm) seam allowance line on the throat plate, remembering to start down a bit to allow for the backtack. With your eye on the ⅜" (1 cm) seam allowance guideline, stitch down to the end of the paper and backtack (A). Remove the paper and check your seam allowance with a hem gauge to make sure you are staying on the line (B).

3 Repeat step 2 with a fresh edge of the paper for the ½" (1.3 cm) seam allowance and the ⅝" (1.6 cm) seam allowance, checking with the hem gauge after each seam line is sewn. Continue to practice until you are comfortable staying on each seam allowance line.

Tip Make sure you are butting the paper up against the line and not covering it or it will be difficult to follow.

Pivot

When you need to change the direction of your stitch line at an angle, you need to pivot. Before lifting the presser foot to turn, it is important to anchor the paper (or fabric) by lowering the needle into it. For this exercise, make a copy of the pivot practice sheet on page 186.

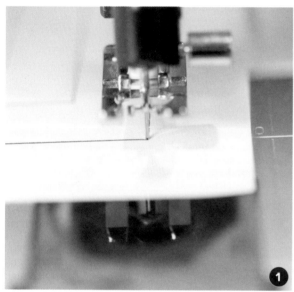

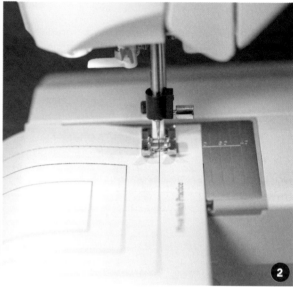

Tip When the beginning and end of your stitching line will meet, rather than back-tack at beginning and end, blend your stitching line by overlapping three stitches.

Directions

1   Line up your paper so that you are starting in the middle of a line for the outer box. Begin by stitching down to the corner of the box and stop with your needle down directly in the corner. It's a good idea to take the last couple of stitches by turning your handwheel toward you so you don't go too far. Leave the needle down in the paper to anchor it in place as you lift the presser foot.

2   Rotate the paper to align with next line of the box. Lower the presser foot.

3   Continue stitching until you reach the next corner, then pivot and repeat until you have stitched all the way around the box and are back where you started. Take three more stitches over the beginning stitches to secure the beginning and end of the line. Turn the handwheel until the take-up lever and needle are at their highest positions, and remove the paper from the machine.

4   Practice on the inner boxes until you feel comfortable with pivoting.

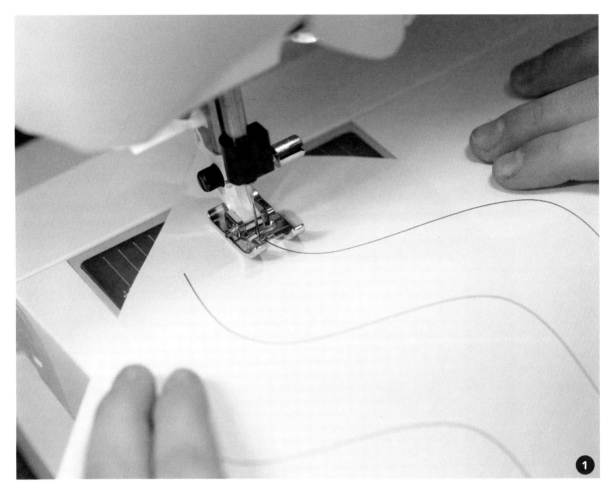

Stitching Curves

Directions

Tip Never lift your presser foot in the middle of a seam without first lowering the needle into the fabric to anchor it. Turn the handwheel toward you until the needle is all the way into the fabric.

1 Make a copy of the slow curve practice sheet (page 186). Start at the beginning of one line and stitch slowly down the line using your hands to steer. The faster you go, the more difficult it will be to stay on the line. These lines are curved gently enough that you should not have to decrease your stitch length, but as the curves get tighter, a shorter stitch length will help you stay on the line. If you stray off the curve, use a series of small pivots to get back on track.

2 Remember to check your holes on the back after each line to see whether you are pushing or pulling too hard.

Scrappy Cards

Once you are comfortable with the practice exercises, thread up your machine and have some fun stitching scraps of fabric to card stock. These creative, free-form cards are fun to make and share.

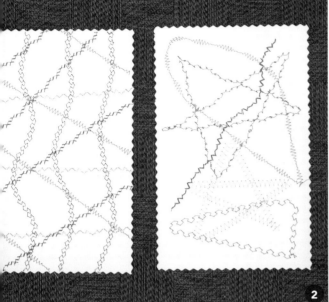

You will need

Tools

- size 80/12 needle
- scissors
- pinking shears

Fabric

- scraps of fabric

Other Supplies

- cotton/polyester thread
- card stock

Directions

1 Thread your machine and ready it for sewing by making sure that the bobbin thread is pulled up and both threads are under the presser foot. Each time you start and stop a seam, check to make sure the take-up lever is in the uppermost position.

2 Cut a 5" x 7" (12.5 x 17.8 cm) piece of card stock. Practice your stitching while making cool designs. Remember: Even though it is paper, you still need to pay attention to the position of the take-up lever and all the basics you just learned to be successful! Backtack at the beginning and end of seams to keep them secure. Try different stitches!

3 Take a 5" x 7" (12.5 x 17.8 cm) piece of card stock and some scraps of fabric. Stitch the scraps of fabric to the card stock. You can overlap fabrics and change threads if you want. You can use your pinking shears to cut the edges of fabric scraps to reduce fraying. Be creative and have some fun!

Techniques you'll need

- How to run your machine
- How to maintain steady hand pressure
- How to sew a straight line
- How to backtack
- How to sew a curved line

You will learn

- How to have a little creative fun

Keep It Close Bed Organizer

Struggling to find your book at night? Need a book light and don't want to get up? Have a thought and want to write it down before you forget? Make a fabulous bedside organizer and have everything at your fingertips! This project is easy to make and easy to modify to your specific needs. Use these techniques to design a locker organizer. Try an appliqué on the pockets!

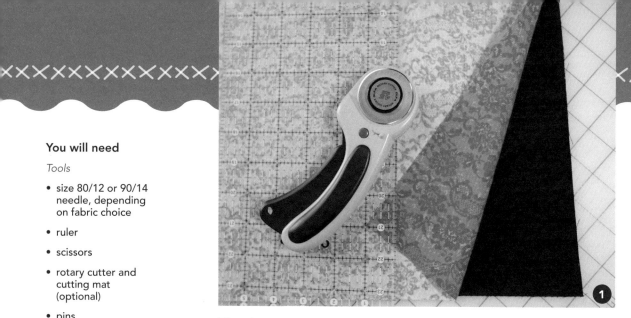

You will need

Tools

- size 80/12 or 90/14 needle, depending on fabric choice
- ruler
- scissors
- rotary cutter and cutting mat (optional)
- pins
- hem gauge
- tailor's chalk or marking pencil
- point turner
- iron
- press cloth
- center guide foot for your machine (optional)
- Hump Jumper (optional)

Fabric

- ¾ yard (69 cm) each of 2 different corduroy or twill fabrics

Other Supplies

- cotton/polyester thread

Directions

Notes: Seam allowances: ½" (1.3 cm) for body of organizer; ¼ (6 mm) for pockets

Choose a sturdy fabric for this to give it the body and strength it will need to hold up to use.

1 Cut one of each from *each* fabric.
   Main piece:
   20" x 36" (51 x 91 cm)
   Pockets:
   6½" x 5" (16.5 x 12.5 cm)
   5" x 6½" (12.5 x 16.5 cm)
   5" x 3" (12.5 x 7.5 cm)
   4" x 5" (10 x 12.5 cm)

(continued)

> **Tip** Lay your fabrics right sides together and cut out fronts and back of organizer and pockets together. They will match better.

Techniques you'll need

- How to cut fabric
- How to pivot
- How to use a point turner
- How to close an opening
- How to trim corners

You will learn

- How to make a self-lined pocket
- How to topstitch

2 Lay the large pieces right sides together and pin around the four sides, leaving an 8" (20 cm) opening to turn.

3 Using a hem gauge, mark dots ½" (1.3 cm) from all four corners as a guide to where to pivot.

4 Start stitching at the double pin at the end of the opening, and stitch to the first corner. To pivot, lower the needle into the dot to anchor the fabric, and then lift the presser foot. Rotate the fabric to turn the corner, lining up the new edge with the ½" (1.3 cm) seam allowance, and lower the presser foot. Continue stitching to the next corner, where you will pivot and repeat until you end up at the beginning of your opening (double pin).

5 To reduce bulk, trim the corners halfway to the pivot point at each corner. This will allow the corners to lay flatter when turned. Reach your hand through the opening and pull the organizer through to turn it right side out.

6 Use a point turner to poke the corners square.

7 Press the seams and organizer flat. At the opening, tuck the seam allowance in and press flat to make a straight edge. Pin in place and stitch the opening closed, stitching close to the folded edge. This is called topstitching. Topstitch the other short end of the organizer a ¼" (6 mm) from the edge. Set aside for later.

8 To make each self-lined pocket, place the matching fabric pieces right sides together and pin around the edges, leaving an opening at the lower edge for turning. Double pin the opening. Just like you did for the body of the organizer, begin at the end of the opening and use a ¼" (6 mm) seam allowance to stitch all the way around pocket, pivoting at the corners and ending at the beginning of the opening. Trim the corners and turn right side out, using the point turner to square the corners. Press the pocket and opening flat (tucking the seam allowance in), but no need to stitch the opening closed. You will do this when you stitch it to the main body of the organizer. Topstitch 1/8" (3 mm) from the upper edge of each pocket. If you have a center guide foot, this is a good time to use it; move the needle over to the left position, and align the guide to the pocket edge.

1 Lay the organizer down with the wrong side facing up and the edge with the stitched opening along the top. Fold the bottom edge up 12" (30.5 cm) so that you can see the right side of the fabric. Mark the center seam line to divide the folded fabric into two pockets.

10 Lay the self-lined pockets on the organizer, placing them where you want but keeping them ¼" (6 mm) away from the center line and 1" (2.5 cm) away from the sides, and with the openings at the bottom. Pin in place, being careful to pin only to the top folded piece of the main organizer, not pinning through to the back two layers.

11 Unfold the body of the organizer and topstitch each pocket in place 1/8" (3 mm) from the edge. Beginning at the upper edge, sew around the edge of the pocket, pivoting at the corners and backtacking at the beginning and end. Do not stitch the top of the pocket!

12 After all the pockets are secured, refold the main body 12" (30.5 cm) up so that the pockets are showing and pin the sides in place. Place pins horizontally across the line marking the center seam.

13 Topstitch two sides together from the top of the flap to the bottom using the edge of the presser foot as a guide. Backtack at beginning and end.

14 Beginning at the folded edge at the bottom of the organizer, stitch along the marked line to divide the body into two large pockets.

Tip
If you double pin the beginning and end of the opening, it will be easy to remember to not stitch there.

Tips Running your point turner along your seam lines from the inside will encourage your seams to lie flat, making it easier at the ironing board.

Tip You can also use a Hump Jumper (yellow tool in the photo) which will help you to stitch over the thick seams and folds.

Secret Pocket Pillow

It's a pillow with a secret zipper pocket. Or it's a messenger bag or laptop bag with a zipper pocket—just add a strap. There are many ways to personalize it: add a big button for a closure, add some appliqués, or sew fringe around the flap.

You will need

Tools

- size 80/12 needle for cotton or one appropriate for your choice of fabric
- measuring tape
- scissors or rotary cutter and mat
- old scissors for cutting zipper
- marking pencil
- pins
- point turner
- iron and press cloth

Fabric

- 1 yard (91 cm) of 45" (114 cm)-wide main fabric (extra fabric for a large or repeat design)
- ½ yard (46 cm) of contrasting fabric for flap
- ½ yard (46 cm) of coordinating fabric or muslin for interior pocket

Other Supplies

- all-purpose thread
- 12" x 18" (30.5 x 46 cm) pillow form
- 14" (35.5 cm) zipper in a matching color
- scrap of fusible interfacing
- button for closure on flap

Techniques you'll need

- How to measure and cut
- How to stitch and pivot
- How to trim corners
- How to topstitch
- How to sew on a button

You will learn

- How to insert a welt pocket zipper
- How to use fusible interfacing to stabilize a buttonhole

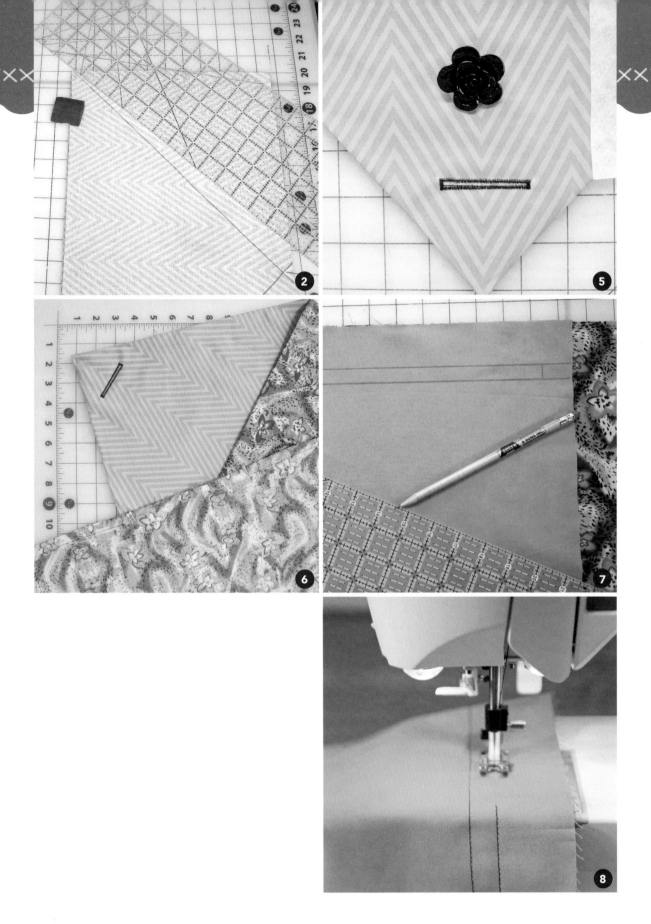

Directions

Notes: Seam allowance: ½" (1.3 cm)

Launder your fabric to preshrink it.

1   Cut the following pieces:
    four 14" x 20" (35.6 x 51 cm) pieces from main fabric
    two 11" x 20" (28 x 51 cm) pieces from flap fabric (you design how much
    flap you want and the shape of the flap)
    two 10" x 16" (25.5 x 40.5 cm) pieces from pocket fabric

2   To make a triangle flap, place the two flap fabric pieces right sides to-
    gether. Mark the center of the 20" (51 cm) side ½" (1.3 cm) from the edge.
    Draw a line from both top corners through the ½" (1.3 cm) mark.

Note
You can design another shape for the flap—curved or straight—if you prefer.

3   Pin along the triangle sides and stitch, leaving the upper edge open and
    backtacking at the beginning and end. Pivot at the point.

4   Cut ½" (1.3 cm) from the stitching line and trim the point to reduce bulk.
    Iron a patch of fusible interfacing in the area of the point where you want a
    buttonhole. Turn right side out through the opening, push out the corners
    with a point turner, and press.

5   Mark a line where you want the buttonhole. It should be slightly longer
    than the button diameter. To make a buttonhole in the flap, see your
    machine for instructions.

6   Place two pillow rectangles right sides together with the triangle sand-
    wiched between them on the wide top edge. Pin the edges, leaving about
    a 5" (12.5 cm) opening for turning. Stitch around the perimeter, using a ½"
    (1.3 cm) seam allowance. Clip the corners, turn right side out, push out the
    corners with a point turner, and press.

7   On one of the remaining two pillow rectangles, place one of the pocket
    rectangles right sides together and centered along a wide edge. Mark a
    line along the pocket 1½" (3.8 cm) from the top edge. Draw another line
    ½" (1.3 cm) below. Mark 1" (2.5 cm) in from each side.

8   Stitch the rectangle, starting in the center of the long line, and reduce
    the stitch length ½" (1.3 cm) from corner, pivot, stitch to the next corner,
    pivot, stitch ½" (1.3 cm) and then return to the regular stitch length and
    continue. Reduce stitch length and pivot at the opposite end; then finish
    stitching the rectangle.

(continued)

9   Cut along the center of the rectangle to within ½" (1.3 cm) of the ends. Clip to the corners, being careful not to clip into the stitches.

10 Pull the pocket out through the opening and press. This will be the zipper opening.

11 Place the zipper underneath, showing through the opening, and pin. With the foot edge aligned against the zipper teeth, topstitch around, stitching close to the edge of the opening, and pivoting at the corners. Carefully walk your needle over the zipper at the ends.

12 Pin the two pocket pieces together and stitch around all four sides. Do not stitch onto the pillow piece.

13 Pin the other pillow piece right sides together to the rectangle with the pocket and stitch around, leaving an opening along the bottom for turning. Trim the corners, turn right side out, push out the corners with a point turner, and press.

14 Pin the two pillow pieces together on the sides and bottom, with the secret pocket on the inside and the triangle flap extending up. Topstitch the three sides, guiding the edge of the presser foot along the pillow edges, being careful to stitch the opening closed at the bottom.

15 Mark the placement for the button and sew it on.

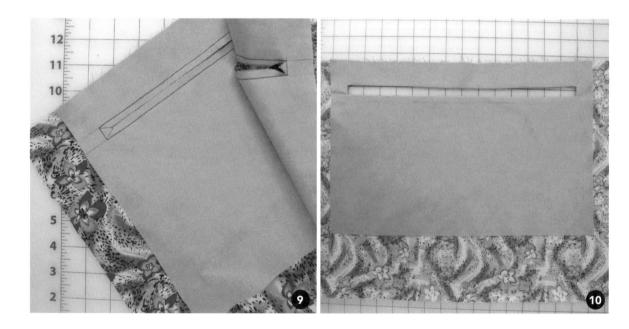

Templates

Straight Stitch Template
Please copy at 200%

―――――――――――――――――
―――――――――――――――――
―――――――――――――――――
―――――――――――――――――
―――――――――――――――――
―――――――――――――――――
―――――――――――――――――

Pivot Template
Please copy at 200%

Slow Curve Template
Please copy at 200%

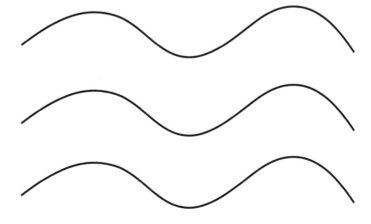

About the Authors

Creative Kids Complete Photo Guide to Bead Crafts

Amy Kopperude is an artist, graphic designer, and editor living in York, Pennsylvania. She grew up in Minnesota among talented family members who supported her creative growth from an early age. Amy is an avid crafter who likes to dabble in all kinds of media and especially enjoys working with small, intricate pieces. She has been creating and designing with beads for many years and occasionally teaches beading workshops for kids and teens. She is also the author of *Bead Bugs: Cute, Creepy, and Quirky Projects to Make with Beads, Wire, and Fun Found Objects*.

Creative Kids Complete Photo Guide to Braiding & Knotting

Sherri Haab is an award-winning, best-selling craft book author, with more than thirty books published to date. She has several DVDs and has appeared on many television networks including HGTV, DIY, JTV, PBS, and local programs. As a certified metal clay instructor, she leads numerous craft and jewelry-making workshops internationally. With her talent for trend spotting and product development, she is known worldwide as an innovator in the craft industry. Her work includes books for children and adults and her own line of craft supplies. She and her husband, Dan, live in Saratoga Springs, Utah. www.sherrihaab.com

Creative Kids Complete Photo Guide to Crochet

Deborah Burger is the author of *Crochet 101* and *How to Make 100 Crochet Appliqués*. She has been teaching crochet for more than 20 years through Girl Scouting, various community centers, summer camps, yarn shops, and the John C. Campbell Folk School. She is active in the online community Ravelry and has written articles and patterns for *Interweave Crochet* and the e-zines, *Crochet Insider* and *Crochet Uncut*. Deb and her musician/potter husband, Don, are the parents of seven grown children and have several grandchildren, most of whom also crochet. In addition to crochet, Deb enjoys knitting, embroidery, painting, fiber sculpture, gardening, performing folk music, and reading.

Creative Kids Complete Photo Guide to Knitting

Mary Scott Huff lives in Fairview, Oregon, and teaches knitting all over the United States. Mary designs knitwear, writes books, blogs, and generally pursues a yarn-centered existence, in a little red house shared with her husband, two children, and two Scottish terriers. Join Mary in her adventures playing with string at www.maryscotthuff.com.

Creative Kids Complete Photo Guide to Sewing

Janith Bergeron, proprietress of Designs by Janith, founded in 1991, specializes in creating beautiful, custom-designed garments. She teaches classes at various sewing-related businesses and schools, striving to bring fun into every stitch and a sense of accomplishment into every project. Janith founded the New Hampshire chapter of the American Sewing Guild in 2001. A Master Certified Sewing Educator-SEA (2008), a Trained Sewing Educator/S&CA since 2002, and a 4-H educator/leader, Janith has been a contributor to *Threads* magazine's Pattern Review since 2003. Janith lives in Barrington, New Hampshire.

Christine Ecker began sewing as a young child with her grandmother. Christine is primarily self-taught, and her sewing interests include specialty dresses, costumes, children's clothes, home decor, crafts, bags, and machine embroidery. As the owner of Stolen Time Creations, Christine worked closely with a local New Hampshire designer creating one-of-a-kind handbags. Christine was an active member of the board for the New Hampshire chapter of the American Sewing Guild. She has been a Trained Sewing Educator/S&CA since 2004. Christine lives in Dover, New Hampshire with her husband and four children. Bella and Freddy Ecker served as hand models for the sewing steps.

Index

Brimming with creative inspiration, how-to projects, and useful information to enrich your everyday life, Quarto Knows is a favorite destination for those pursuing their interests and passions. Visit our site and dig deeper with our books into your area of interest: Quarto Creates, Quarto Cooks, Quarto Homes, Quarto Lives, Quarto Drives, Quarto Explores, Quarto Gifts, or Quarto Kids.

© 2021 Quarto Publishing Group USA Inc.

First Published in 2021 by Quarry Books, an imprint of The Quarto Group, 100 Cummings Center, Suite 265-D, Beverly, MA 01915, USA.
T (978) 282-9590 F (978) 283-2742 QuartoKnows.com

The contents of this book were previously published in the following titles from Quarry Books' Creative Kids series:
Complete Photo Guide to Bead Crafts © 2015
Complete Photo Guide to Braiding and Knotting © 2016
Complete Photo Guide to Crochet © 2015
Complete Photo Guide to Knitting © 2015
Complete Photo Guide to Sewing © 2015

Quarry Books titles are also available at discount for retail, wholesale, promotional, and bulk purchase. For details, contact the Special Sales Manager by email at specialsales@quarto.com or by mail at The Quarto Group, Attn: Special Sales Manager, 100 Cummings Center, Suite 265-D, Beverly, MA 01915, USA.

10 9 8 7 6 5 4 3 2 1

ISBN: 978-0-7603-7092-6

Digital edition published in 2021
eISBN: 978-0-7603-7093-3

Library of Congress Cataloging-in-Publication Data can be found under the original titles, listed above.

Cover Design: Mattie Wells
Series Design: Laura McFadden

Printed in China